HELPING EMPLOYEES DEVELOP JOB SKILL
A Casebook of Training Approaches

HELPING EMPLOYEES DEVELOP JOB SKILL

A Casebook of Training Approaches

by
JAMES E. GARDNER

The Bureau of National Affairs, Inc. Washington, D.C.

Library of Congress Cataloging in Publication Data

Gardner, James E
  Helping employees develop job skill.

  Bibliography: p. 175
  Includes index.
  1. Employees, Training of. I. Title.
HF5549.5.T7G33   658.31'243   76-44483
ISBN 0-87179-227-3

Printed in the United States of America
International Standard Book Number: 0-87179-227-3

To Annie and Dode

Preface

Those of us who have responsibility for the training of employees are in the business of helping people develop job skill quickly and efficiently. It is evident to me that we have not gone far enough nor have we been discriminating enough in carrying out this objective.

Perhaps our very success, small as it often has been, has gotten in our way. We have discovered that a systematic approach to training, whatever it consists of, is likely to be an improvement over a haphazard approach or no approach at all; it is superior at least to a reliance upon the employee himself picking up job skills by trial and error. Since it does work (up to a point) or has once worked, we continue to put our faith in it, whatever it is. More than this, we build it into a rigid procedure, enshrining for all eternity, for example, the four-step JIT (Job Instruction Training) procedure or endowing the methods statement and the stop watch with mysterious powers of eliciting and shaping the trainee's responses.

The factory supervisor needs more help than our static and oversimplified procedures afford him. A more comprehensive view of job learning is in order—and a more comprehensive view of how we can arrange to expedite that learning through its various stages on the climb to job competency. Moreover, a closer and more diagnostic look at the needs of the individual trainee as he makes the climb is indicated.

I have tried in this book to treat the job-learning process in a realistically broad way, to discuss it as the developing thing it is, and to make a balanced statement of training approaches appropriate or useful not only early in the training but at those crucial stages when the employee moves close to job competency or is faced (particularly at times of change) with the problem of maintaining it.

And I have attempted to provide the supervisor with background information on learning and related training approaches and with the opportunity, through discussion and role-playing, to see applications—so that perhaps he will be in better position to carry out his training responsibilities on the job itself with discrimination and insight and will strengthen his own knowledge of how to deal differently with training problems that are not alike, training stages that are not alike, and trainees who are not alike.

I wish to thank Fieldcrest Mills, Inc., for permission to use certain materials from a copyrighted Fieldcrest manual I had prepared for the training of job instructors.

J. E. G.

Eden, N.C.
1976

Table of Contents

Part 1
BACKGROUND

Introduction

The objective of job training is to enable an employee to perform his job in such a way as to meet the standards of output, quality, waste control, safety, and other operational requirements. In short, the objective is job competency or mastery in its various operational phases. Of major concern are output (or efficiency) and quality requirements.

Requirements are usually based on cost considerations, primarily on a determination of standard labor cost per unit of output. If these costs are exceeded, that is, if the trainee's output is less than the industrially engineered standard, the trainee is not demonstrating a mastery of the job in a practical sense. Similarly, if he produces too many defective items or too much waste, he is not displaying job competency. It is this strict operational definition of the outcome of learning that the supervisor must live with. And it is this definition which should guide our training. Our training should have the objective of enabling the employee to perform at the level required to meet job standards; and the "terminal behavior" indicating that the learning has occurred should be the actual performance of the employee at this level. In short, the *objective* of job training is *to enable the employee to meet job standards*. The *criterion* or indication of the success of the training is that *he meets the job standards in actual performance*.

There are circumstances, however, which may stand in the way of job competency or prevent evidence of it from appearing. It is possible for the trainee, for example, to reach the required level of skill but not produce at that level. As will be discussed later, factors other than learning (such as adverse job conditions beyond the employee's control or self-imposed limitations on output) may influence job performance. In addition, not every trainee placed in a particular job classification has the capacity to achieve job skill at the level required to satisfy job

3

standards. This situation occurs especially in complex or multi-task jobs. At the advanced stages of progress such jobs may place demands on certain aptitudes in which an individual trainee may be somewhat weak. We are often faced with such a problem in a tight labor market.

These difficulties should not lead us, as supervisors or as trainers assisting the supervisor, to abandon the supervisor's objectives. They do suggest the wisdom of modifying our goals to the extent of striving for what is realistically within our power to accomplish. We should attempt, with the best training resources and approaches at our disposal, to bring trainees to a point where they can truly run the job, or as close to this point as their individual capabilities permit, with the hope that no serious conflict occurs during the training period between their true level of acquired skill and their actual performance, between the "can" and the "do."

Since validly established job standards are likely to be unyielding or capable of only slight bending, if a company is to control costs and remain profitable, the trainer's most realistic course is to accept the necessary conditions and the available trainees and to strive in a mature and insightful way to meet the supervisor's operational objectives. In this endeavour, the use of foreshortened, oversimplified, rigid, and misconceived training efforts will not serve. What, then, will?

Bringing employees to a high level of skill is a long developmental process that depends upon an adequate start; a shaping, refining, and quickening of perceptions and responses; an integrating and combining of job parts; and, perhaps above all else, a diagnostic approach to identifying individual difficulties of trainees at various stages of learning. This is not to say that the developmental nature of job learning is not duplicated in other types of learning. But one must be wary of applying to job-skills training the sorts of simplified statements of objective and criteria which can be derived from many types of verbal or academic learning. In industrial training we are not teaching an employee to solve an equation, or to distinguish between an adverb and an adjective, or to trace the earthworm's digestive processes. While there are degrees of skill or proficiency in this sort of learning, the developmental process usually need not go very far to meet the objective. The process usually can be completed for the limited purpose at hand by a classroom period or training "session" of a certain length or by a series of a certain number of programmed frames (if programmed instruction is used). The specific item of knowledge or short-cycle act of skill is "learned" usually for short retention and rather immediate playback, and that's that.

In contrast, the acquisition of job skill goes on and on. The trainee's pattern of responses must be shaped and sharpened, must be speeded, must take on the economy of habit; skill in the performance of the individual tasks or subparts must be fitted together to permit mastery of the full workload or job assignment. These shaping and quickening and integrating processes continue over a relatively long period of time. It is naive and quite unrealistic to expect that a classroom type of exercise or a so-called training session or a simple four-step procedure will produce the required degree of job skill and endow a trainee with genuine competency in his job. They are a start at best. The training job is not completed until the trainer does whatever is necessary, using sound instruction arrangements and techniques, to move the individual trainee through the long learning process, progressively improving his performance to an acceptable level of skill or to that level which is at the top of his capacity.

Individual differences are important in job learning and should be taken into account as we determine the kinds of training approaches and the extent of training efforts needed for efficient development of skill. We cannot expect to march all trainees along to the same degree of accomplishment within the same period of time or to enjoy equal success with the same approaches from one trainee to another. Our specific measures should be geared to the needs of the individual trainee as he progresses from one learning stage to another. In short, the development of job skill requires employee-centered procedures rather than strict adherence to a fixed program.

Of course, there are intermediate objectives (discussed in Chapter 10) relating primarily to the performance of separate tasks of the full job. That is, at certain stages the trainee should be able to perform a task consistently by the approved method or to perform it within a certain time limit. The indications of success, however, cannot be restricted to a short sample of performance at elementary or intermediate levels of skill. If the progressive nature of skill-acquisition is to guide our training, we must assist the trainee to attain increasingly difficult goals, must prepare the way for the next stage in the evolving process, and must assure that the learning of the full job genuinely occurs. That the employee has gone through the task a few times is not sufficient evidence of job learning—may not even be evidence of a good start.

The attainment of intermediate goals, however well set, does not provide a proof of or unfailing prediction of ultimate job learning. A job is more than an arithmetical accumulation of parts. A trainee may meet stringent performance requirements in all of the separate parts or tasks of a job and yet be unable to run the full job with satisfactory skill. To meet the final objective, the trainee must bring all of the parts together and acquire skill in the integrating or organizational phase of job performance. He must finally run the *total* job competently, at the level of skill required to meet operational standards.

The type of training characterized by short-range objectives and related measurements, which concentrates on the beginning phase of learning and ignores or subordinates its evolving aspects, is not an adequate answer to the need of untrained employees. Training must be a long-term effort to help the individual through the long and involved process of job learning—in short, to help him to *develop* job skill.

Chapter 1

The Acquisition of Job Skill

Job learning—the acquisition of skill in the performance and integration of job tasks—is hard to define, but it has a shape that can be described to some extent. Through experience, an employee is able to do something he could not do before. A change occurs in his behavior, a change which is due neither to physical developments only (maturing or aging, for example) nor to temporary emotional states. That is, the employee can repeat the act and, if the conditions for retention are favorable, he can continue to perform it more or less indefinitely.

The change in behavior wrought by learning basically involves new linkings of stimuli and responses. The hooking-up of a response to a stimulus to form a new combination may be achieved in its simplest form by means of conditioning procedures. An established response may be connected with a new stimulus if the new stimulus is presented at the same time as the old. Or a new response may be attached to a stimulus if the learner is rewarded in some way (is reinforced, that is) upon making the response.

This elemental pattern is evident in job learning, as a form of learning; the employee is enabled to make new responses to old stimuli and old responses to new stimuli. Viewed in the large context of a job and expressed in job-related terms, the process is one in which the employee is enabled to recognize specific signals calling for specific actions and is enabled to perform the acts. The particular couplings of signals and actions will be new to his experience but within his capacity to accomplish.

Let us look at examples of stimuli and responses in the performance of actual job tasks. When his stock runs low, the ma-

7

chine operator takes steps to replenish it. When a sign of mechanical malfunctioning appears, the machine repairman begins his diagnostic or repairing procedures. A perception is involved in the linking-up process; it might be considered an intermediate or mediating response which precedes the overt (or manipulating) response. For example, the operator first perceives that the supply of stock is at a certain level before he makes a move to add to it. The repairman similarly must perceive the evidence of malfunctioning before responding with corrective measures.

Generalizing may occur with learning. That is, the operator or repairman may come to apply the same response to a number of stimuli. The repairman, for instance, may find that the same trouble-shooting procedures may serve to clear up several symptoms of mechanical difficulties.

In the learning of industrial tasks, however, discrimination is probably a more important objective and outcome of learning than is generalization. The operator will note the level of the stock with a "discriminating eye." If the stock level is high he makes no replenishing response; it would be pointless or inefficient. If the supply is exhausted or extremely low, his replenishing response may be too late; the machine may stop or the process flow may be interrupted. Part of his learning consists of tying his supply-replenishing response to rather specific indications (in this case, the stock at a certain narrowly defined level); this response is called forth by one condition or situation but not by others.

The role of discrimination among stimuli in the learning process is perhaps more clearly seen in the case of the repairman. By sight, hearing, and feeling, or by a combination of sensory means, he detects the evidence of malfunctioning (as distinct from the evidences of acceptable operation) and makes a distinction among malfunctions of various types, involving different mechanical motions or subassemblies. Diagnosis begins with a discrimination among stimuli.

Discrimination must occur among the responses as well as the stimuli. As he learns a job task, the employee retains the responses that pay off in terms of accomplishment and eliminates the unproductive responses. The machine operator may know when to replenish the stock, but his learning of the task is incomplete unless he establishes the responses which will enable him to fill the supply bin or magazine, hopefully in an efficient way. The repairman may detect the need for the repair of a particular mechanical motion, but his learning must go forward to establish the responses which will cure the trouble.

Of course, the learning process in industrial tasks is a much more complex matter than a simple stimulus-response model would suggest. We are concerned with a multiplicity of stimuli and responses making up a long series or pattern of activity. One stimulus does not serve to send an employee through the lengthy and intricate series of motions required to complete a task. An unfolding array of stimuli will guide his responses as he proceeds. The employee builds a complex chain of stimulus-response links which propel him through the entire task repeatedly. The beginning stimulus triggers the employee's first response, and the employee moves through the rest of the task by sequentially making the "right" responses to the "right" stimuli as these stimuli are revealed or presented. The perceived effect of the first response provides a stimulus for the second response; the effect of the second response, a stimulus for the third, etc.

The stimulus presented by the response is usually in the form of a detectable effect of the response on the material being processed. That is, the employee makes a certain move with his hands or tool and what shows up, as a result, at the point of contact with the material becomes the stimulus for the next response. Perception, of course, is required in this process. In executing the full cycle from response to succeeding response, the employee takes a certain action; it has an effect; he perceives that effect; and on that basis he proceeds to the next action.

The stimulus may become "internalized" as skill develops; in such a case the movement involved in the response itself carries the signal for the next response. If he has achieved a high level of skill, the trainee picks up this signal. He no longer needs to look at the material to perceive how his response has worked out; for this perception the skilled employee may rely on the kinesthetic sense—the sensations from the muscles in-

volved in the movement itself. If "the feel is right," he knows
the effect on the material is "right"—without otherwise not-
ing—and proceeds to his next action.

Characteristics of Learning Stages

Since the learning process itself is so difficult to define, it
would be prudent (and useful as well, fortunately) to discuss
learning from a descriptive point of view. We are on firm
ground if we try merely to describe the characteristics of the
learners or of their performance at various stages of learning—
that is, if we simply report what we can observe about the learners and their activities as they acquire skill.

In the complete process of skill-acquisition the trainee
moves from a rough approximation of the task, involving main-
ly the sequence of steps, to a smooth, quick, and precise pattern
of motions which is performed with a minimum of conscious
attention. We are not quite sure how he gets there, but we do
know that he works his way through intermediate stages that
we can identify.[1]

He comes to know what to attend to as he begins the task
and moves through it and what sensory channels (vision, hearing, feel, or whatever) to use in attending. He has ideas about
how things should go (some of which he brings into the job
from past experience), ideas that are modified by him as the result of the successes or failures of his efforts. He begins to make
a distinction between the stimuli (signals or cues) that require
attention and response on his part and those he can ignore. He
begins to make distinctions between responses (moves and acts
of various sorts) that bring results and those that do not. In
summary, he begins to detect the signs that will guide him
through the task, that will tell him how well his responses work;
and his responses begin to work better, to produce the signs of
correctness.

Sometimes he develops little verbal habits that he uses as
crutches to connect up the signals and the responses. For ex-

---

[1]For detailed discussions of stages or phases in the development of skill, see W.
Douglas Seymour, INDUSTRIAL SKILLS (London: Pitman, 1966), pp. 145–153; Paul M.
Fitts, *Perceptual-Motor Skill Learning*, in Arthur W. Melton (ed.), CATEGORIES OF HUMAN
LEARNING (New York: Academic Press, 1964), pp. 261–268.

ample, if the top light of a panel display requires him to stop the machine, he might use the rhyme "light at top, machine stop." These aids eventually tend to drop out, and the trainee finally goes directly to the right action without such promptings.

Gradually he becomes much sharper at spotting how well he is doing, at using his senses to pick up the signs, and at attaching the correct meaning to them. His perception is both quicker and surer. He picks up the signs in a hurry and gets meaning from them in a hurry, and on the basis of his information he proceeds to the next step in the series of motions or makes necessary adjustments or corrections before continuing, thus quickening and sharpening his responses. In addition, his perceptions appear to take on a certain economy. He seems to make do with fewer signs; he goes directly to the heart of the matter. Sometimes he does not even wait for the signs in their full revelation but anticipates outcomes from one stage of his progression through the task to another.

Finally, the process becomes "automatic." The employee works through the task apparently with little conscious attention; but he maintains, nevertheless, a basic alertness to errors or deviations that call back into play an exercise of conscious attention for their correction.

Shift to Reliance on Different Abilities as Learning Progresses

The stages just described seem to be parts of the pattern by which skill is developed. The acquisition of skill is not a clear-cut process, however. Stages overlap, for example. And there are differences between trainees and between job tasks in regard to the way skills are acquired.

Many tasks require, for efficient performance, stages during which the trainee moves from a dependence on a certain combination of abilities to dependence on a modified combination.[2] Industrial trainers have known for years how trainees, as they progress toward mastery, proceed from a reliance on

---

[2]For a short, summary statement of Fleishman's findings on abilities contributing to performance at various stages of practice, see Edwin A. Fleishman, *Human Abilities and the Acquisition of Skill*, in Edward A. Bilodeau (ed.), ACQUISITION OF SKILL (New York: Academic Press, 1966), pp. 158–163.

visual attention to the various cues to a reliance on the "feel" of things, on information fed back through the sense of touch and through the kinesthetic sense. In tasks in which an advance to a higher level of skill requires a shift from vision to feel, the trainee apparently must be "trained" to a point of confidence in the kinesthetic feedback before he will give up his reliance on vision as his major sensory channel.

We also know by observation of trainees that a multi-machine or multi-task assignment will, at the later stages of learning, require the trainee to put the parts and elements of the job together, that is, to organize the job in such a way as to permit advance planning, preventive actions, establishment of priorities, and so forth. In general, he must learn at the end to "stay on top of" the job.

Only a few abilities are involved in these most obvious shifts which we have used for illustration—that is, (1) the shift from vision to the kinesthetic sense for perceptual feedback and (2) the shift of emphasis from the manipulative performance of separate tasks, involving dexterity as the primary ability, to the organization of the full job and its accompanying dependence on abilities to plan and coordinate. In a particular job the shifts may involve other abilities; but, whatever the specific abilities, the general conclusion seems to hold up: The combination of abilities associated with performance will differ from one stage of learning to another.

The Measure and Shape of Learning

Performance as a Measure of Learning

However it occurs, we measure learning primarily by means of an index of performance. Performance is not a pure or exclusive measure of learning. Other factors affect performance, and some learning occurs which is not directly measurable. But in industrial tasks, performance (in units of output, quality indices, etc.) is the most useful measure of learning; it is the objective of a wide variety of efforts (selection, incentive systems, supervisory actions, etc.), chief among which is training itself. We can reasonably assume that, in most instances, any significant amount of learning will show up in the performance of the employee.

With experienced employees who are being retrained in revised job methods, particularly when a change in workload or piece-rate is impending, the effects of learning may not be so clearly evident. They may be masked or submerged so that they do not show up significantly in performance. Restriction of output is not an uncommon occurrence in these circumstances. With trainees new to the job, however, those performance measures which are valid indices of job mastery may be used with some confidence as measures of learning. In most instances they will tell us if the trainee is learning and to what extent.

The Learning Curve as a View of Progress in Learning

A condensed view of the learning process is given by the so-called learning curve, which plots the progress of trainees in measurable units. The learning curve, as reflected in measures of job performance (units of production, for example), is typically a negatively accelerated curve. That is, there is less gain each day or week (or whatever time interval is used in the plotting). Usually the trainee starts off pretty fast. There is much to learn and he does not begin from scratch. His past experience helps him in most cases; he already can make the individual motions and some of the combinations of motions which are part of the method of the new job. He progressively finds less to be learned, and he usually encounters greater difficulties in mastering the diminishing remainder, especially the more precise or complex aspects. Consequently, the units gained in each succeeding period tend to become fewer.

The plateaus that show up as periods of little or no progress in the learning curve are a disturbing problem in skill development. Fortunately, a "true" plateau, one essential to the learning process and therefore inescapable, is possibly rarer than supposed in the past. Its genuineness or inevitability has come under strong doubt. Certainly it appears to be influenced by the sort of measurement we use or by our failure to control the conditions of learning. As indicated earlier, performance indices may not be a sensitive measure of learning progress in its various aspects. In addition, the intervals of measurement will affect the shape of the curve. More importantly (as will be discussed more fully later), we invite "false" plateaus or prolong the duration of plateaus by making certain instructional errors or employing unwise training arrangements.

Finally, it should be kept in mind that motor skills improve gradually over a great number of repetitions. The curve, therefore, will tend to keep climbing by very small increments over a long period of time.

Chapter 2

Retention of Job Skill

Industrial trainers are concerned not only with original learning but with retention of what is learned. Obviously, the length of the training period itself will depend on the time required to assure retention. We want the trainee to take his learning into the job and to hold onto it.

Fortunately, it has been found that motor skills, if genuinely learned, stay with a person for a long time. Losses of such skill are not very pronounced even over relatively long periods of nonpractice, and the skill can be strengthened in rather short order.

Retention is influenced by a number of factors, but two of them appear to exert the largest influence. These are:

- the level or strength of original learning
- the interference of other learning.

Effect of Original Learning and Interference

Retention studies have uncovered a significant connection between the amount of learning retained and the strength of original learning. Where the individual's learning level is high, the retention level tends to be high.[1] The lesson to industrial trainers is obvious.

When there is a loss of skill after original learning, the important consideration (beyond the level of learning itself) is not so much the passage of time alone but what happens in the intervening time. What does the trainee do in the time between "learning" the task and returning to it?

---

[1] Edwin A. Fleishman, *Human Abilities and the Acquisition of Skill*, in Edward A. Bilodeau (ed.), ACQUISITION OF SKILL (New York: Academic Press, 1966), pp. 163–164.

The best assurance of retention apparently comes through sleep (or complete inactivity) in the interim period. Sleep immediately after the learning experience (even if followed by waking activity) appears to be associated with substantial retention.[2] Waking activity after the learning experience apparently exerts an unfavorable influence on retention, that is, interferes with the previous learning.

The unfortunate fact is that some learning interferes with other learning (although perhaps this is not so powerful a factor in motor learning as we may have thought earlier). The interference may go backward (retroactive interference) or forward (proactive interference). Learning A may interfere with the learning of B (proactive). Learning B may interfere with the retention of A (retroactive).

The interference seems to occur primarily when A and B are somewhat similar to each other (not the same and not dissimilar). In automobile driving, the learning of the automatic shift is disturbed by our old habits developed in manipulating the straight shift. If we go back to a straight shift we have difficulties. In industrial operations, interference can be observed when a new task to be learned has the appearance of the old but is performed differently. An example is the operation of a new machine which looks like the old but requires different procedures and methods to run it. That is, the signals to do something (the stimuli) are the same but the doing (the responses) must be different. In the new task we know when to do things, but the things are different and we get fouled up by our old responses.

The interference seems to be strongest when the task involves opposed responses—for example, having to move a lever backward instead of forward to stop the machine or having to reverse the positions of parts in an assembly operation. The old habit of responses interferes with the development of the new, and the competition is especially strong if the task requires a reversal of movements or motion patterns.

The meaningfulness of the response·is another consid-

---

[2] See Bernard Berelson and Gary A. Steiner, HUMAN BEHAVIOR, AN INVENTORY OF SCIENTIFIC FINDINGS (New York: Harcourt, Brace and World, 1964), pp. 133–168, for a summary including this and other findings from learning research studies.

eration. Apparently the more meaningful the old response, the more it tends to interfere with the learning of the new. Old and meaningful habits which have served a clear and useful purpose for a long time are extremely hard to shake and tend to "repulse" the new.

On the other hand, the learning of one task can help us learn another task. Such facilitation seems to occur when the new task presents us with new signals (stimuli) but requires the same set of responses. That is, we already know what to do and only have to "catch on" to the new signs telling us to go ahead. In short, the stimuli are different, the responses the same. The machine, for example, may have a new signaling arrangement telling the employee when the raw stock needs replenishing or the finished piece is to be removed or when certain mechanical difficulties arise, but the employee's procedure in each of these situations is unchanged. Since the operator already knows what to do, he has several legs up on the new task. All he has to do is to learn the new set of signals—the easier part of the battle.

Other Arrangements Influencing Retention

Aside from the factors of interference and the level of original learning, there are a number of other arrangements or conditions of learning which affect retention, among them:

1. In learning verbal material, active recitation helps retention, although the advantage of recitation is reduced if the material is highly meaningful.

2. Meaningfulness itself is a factor in retention (as well as in original learning.) We tend to remember meaningful material. As an exercise to illustrate the effect of meaningfulness, try this: Memorize a list of 12 nonsense syllables, of three letters each, having no meaning at all. Then memorize twelve words of three letters each (dog, rat, ate, etc.). Then memorize 12 words of three letters each which can be strung into a meaningful story (dog, ate, rat, etc.). Compare learning difficulties and retention.

3. The serial position of memorized material also exerts an influence on retention. The items at the end and be-

ginning of a series tend to be retained better than the middle items.

4. What is learned through spaced practice is generally (though not always) retained longer than learning acquired through massing of practice.

The Transfer of Training

A problem at the heart of industrial training is how to assure that what an employee learns in the training period and under training arrangements can be applied to the job—that is, how to provide for a maximum transfer to the job of the skills and knowledge he has picked up in training. The question, expressed still another way, is whether the learning we bring about in the trainee through our training efforts is a genuine preparation (or the most efficient preparation) for running the actual job.

We would not prepare a man to operate a machine on the job by teaching him to drive spikes with a sledge hammer during the training period. Expertness with the sledge hammer certainly does not endow a man with expertness on the machine-operating job. The idea of a transfer of skills between such dissimilar tasks is clearly absurd. But we often make the mistake of expecting such transfer when the tasks are similar.

The very similarity is often the problem, as we have seen in our discussion of interference. If during training the employee develops skill in a task that resembles the actual job task, the training may be a handicap to him when he goes on the job, particularly if he has to use a somewhat different set of responses to accomplish the actual job task. Even when facilitation occurs—when the response patterns (the "how to do it") are the same from training to job and only the signals to do things (control board, gauges, buttons, lights, etc.) are different—the question of efficient use of training time is still present. Transfer of the pattern of responses alone is, of course, important. But how can we assure an even greater transfer, involving virtually the whole bundle?

The evidence from research investigations of transfer of skills provides a few ideas for our guidance. Although not absolute, the indications are that:

- Identical elements are capable of transfer.
- Principles or concepts are capable of transfer.

When the task or subtask taught in the training situation is the same as on the job—involves the same signals to do things and same methods for doing them—the skill developed in training could be expected to transfer to the job. When the principles or concepts or rules applying to the training tasks apply to the job tasks as well, the trainee, if his training in the principles has been adequate, can be expected to use the principles as an aid in mastering the job tasks. Let us take, for example, the training on machines which are somewhat different from the actual production machines. If certain problems of product quality are associated with certain conditions of the machines used for training purposes and if the same relationship between quality and machine conditions is true also of the production machines, the trainee is in position to apply the finding to the job. Or if certain machine settings (or combinations) will remedy a particular malfunction on both the training machine and the production machine, again the situation is right for transfer. In the case of the training of machine repairmen, the transferable principles may be the basic principles of mechanics or physics utilized by both the training machine and production machine in common. One could list as rules or principles or concepts on most jobs a whole series of relationships between causes and results (in terms of operational effects involving quality, waste, efficiency, malfunctioning, etc.)

There is some evidence supporting the point of view that principles are better retained if the trainee is permitted to evolve them on his own. Since the amount to be learned on most jobs is considerable and will include a number of principles, we can ill afford the time required by the trainee to work through a series of trial-and-error efforts to derive the applicable rules by himself. It would be perhaps a more economical procedure to "give" him the principles and use other means of assuring understanding and retention.

Where there are identical elements and common principles capable of transfer from the training situation to the job itself, we cannot be positive that the transfer will occur automatically. The trainee needs help, and so the question for the trainer is: What help can be given? What can be done to maximize transfer? And, in connection with our earlier discussion, what can be done about interference? Indeed, about basic learning and retention themselves, the fundamental objectives to which interference and transfer relate?

The Problem: Apply the Knowledge About Learning States and Retention

The task of the industrial trainer (who is the supervisor himself or by delegation is carrying out the supervisor's responsibility) is to bring about learning efficiently and to maximize retention. The usefulness of a knowledge of how learning occurs—or, at least, of the stages the learner passes through—lies in the prospect it opens up to us for expediting the process and the clues it suggests for doing it. How can we assist the trainee to progress from one stage to another and finally arrive at the kind of job performance which represents a high order of skill?

Without claiming absolute answers, we can with reasonable confidence expect that certain arrangements and conditions under which instruction is given will help the process along. And we can also expect that certain ways in which the instruction is given—the teaching techniques themselves—will work to the trainee's advantage. Similarly, knowledge of retention, even limited knowledge, puts us in better position to identify and use certain arrangements and instructional procedures which will help the trainee retain what he has learned.

The rest of this book will therefore explore a number of arrangements and techniques which appear to contribute to the learning and retention of job skills and knowledge. And through the use of cases for discussion and role-playing taken from industrial experience, it will attempt to illustrate for the trainer and supervisor how and when these approaches may be applied.

Part 2

ARRANGEMENTS FOR LEARNING

Introduction

A supervisor or job instructor would be foolish to try to instruct a trainee without regard to the circumstances under which the instruction is given. The necessity for preparation is obvious, and such preparation should include the setting-up of conditions and arrangements under which the training is most likely to pay off.

We mean such commonplace matters as these: What exactly should the instructor teach and how much of it should he teach at a time? When should he teach it and how much time should he spend on it? What should he teach it with—that is, what materials and equipment or machinery should he use? Unless these issues are resolved, the instructor may be going through the motions to little avail because he is putting too heavy a burden on the instructional techniques themselves. These techniques cannot be expected to carry the whole load of instruction alone if learning and retention are our objectives.

The arrangements, to begin with, should be such as to increase the probabilities of learning and retention. They should constitute a framework which itself will serve to reduce some of the obstacles to learning and retention (such as interference) and will increase the extent to which learned skills are transferred to the job itself.

Fortunately, we have a number of guides for setting up arrangements conducive to learning. We will examine them in the next three chapters.

Chapter 3

How Much to Teach at One Time

How much of the job should a trainee practice? Unless the job involves only one very simple task and the answer is therefore somewhat obvious, this is the key question in the scheduling of training. It should be resolved in the light of the relative advantages to learning of training in the "whole" and training in "parts."

How much the trainee should tackle at one time will depend somewhat upon what is to be learned and who is doing the learning. If the task is short and rather gross in nature, is highly meaningful, or is tightly fitted together, one motion flowing into the other through a short sequence of motions, the evidence seems to favor learning the whole operation at once. On the other hand, learning by parts appears to be the superior approach if the task is long, or complex, or has aspects of precision and exactness in it, or is loosely strung together. If the trainee's learning capacity is large, he will tend to learn the job more quickly in large chunks. If he is a slow learner, it is best to feed him a little at a time. His prior experience in learning—the way he has usually gone about his learning chores and the kind of learning requirements he has been exposed to—may also exert an influence on the size of learning dose that best suits him now.

The amount to be practiced will also depend upon other arrangements for learning and the stage of learning the trainee is in. Specifically, the "whole" method seems to go along well with practice which is broken up and spaced out (see Chapter 4 for a discussion of distributed practice). And it appears to take on advantages as practice proceeds and the trainee moves toward mastery of the task.

There is some merit, apparently, in breaking the job into small units, concentrating most of the practice time on the difficult parts in the early stages of training, and then combining the parts for "whole" practice later. But as indicated, the wisdom of the approach will depend upon the success of the individual trainee; and it is on this basis that the instructor should modify his attack. It may be better to start out with fairly large segments as a sort of exploratory or diagnostic gesture to detect which particular parts will cause difficulty for the individual trainee and then to give special practice in these parts before recombining.

Underlying our decision in this matter should be the view that success is important to learning. The task should be large enough to add up to a new and unique pattern of motions requiring genuine learning on the part of the trainee, but it should not be so large as to prevent a significant measure of success early in the learning period.

If we go to extremes in breaking a task into parts, we run the danger of reducing the task to parts so small that they become meaningless to the trainee, who sees little accomplished by them. Furthermore, they are extremely difficult to bring together in an attempted performance of the full task. A time-study element is a part of this size, large enough to time accurately but usually too small for training purposes.

It would be foolhardy to go even further, that is, to break the task into moves, reaches, and other elementary methods segments for separate practice. Aside from the difficulties of connecting them, the extent to which these minute segments are trainable is open to question. Practice apparently has little effect on the speed of reaches or moves, for example; most new employees can already accomplish such motions nearly as well as they ever will. Practice, however, can increase the speed with which we *position* or *grasp* or *select* (the manipulations required at the beginning or end of the reach or move). But we would not begin even with these manipulative elements because they are just too small. If they are separated out at all, they should be separated only when a diagnostic look revealed that, within a genuine training task, there were hold-ups and fumbles in these subparts. In such instance the subpart should be fitted back into the larger pattern of motions before it becomes rigidly established as an isolated unit of skill.

The problem with learning in parts is that connections must be established later in the learning process; the disadvantage of learning by wholes is that the experience of early success is often beyond the reach of the trainee. Parts give the trainee the experience of early success; wholes establish the connections early.

An approach which combines the advantages of parts and wholes is the so-called progressive-part method. In this method the trainee picks up new parts one at a time, but he combines practice in the part previously learned with practice in the new part. The trainee practices part A, then part B combined with part A, then part C combined with parts A and B. This approach is a natural one in a continuing task of a sort which requires successful completion of one part before the employee can proceed to the next; many industrial tasks are such as to lend themselves to this kind of attack. By this method the trainee can experience early success since he tackles only one part at a time, and he builds in the connections as he goes along by means of practice in the progressive combination of parts.

Many jobs are concerned with continuous-process operations which cannot be interrupted in order to break the job into repeatable tasks of a size most conducive to learning. If training must be done on the job itself and in the regular routine of processing the materials, this limitation is likely to prolong the training period and increase the required amount of explanation and demonstration in view of the restriction on practice in units which the trainee can encompass. But the idea of breaking the job into training tasks need not be abandoned. We can still concentrate on segments of the job, catching them as they occur, and build up skill progressively, task by task, until the total job is mastered.

Let us say that tasks A, B, and C comprise the total job, are too heavy a burden for the trainee to carry in full from the start, and must be learned as they come up in the regular routine. The trainee's practice can begin early in A, but the instructor can continue the explanation and demonstration of B and C (as he himself performs these latter tasks.) Then we can extend the trainee's practice to B along with A while the instructor continues his demonstration and performance of C. And finally we can give the trainee practice in the whole operation.

Consideration of task difficulty and learner motivation may suggest the advisability of hopping about a bit without regard to the operational sequence (like starting with B and then moving to A or C). But in many instances our arrangements can adopt the progressive-part procedure; that is, we can start with the first task in the regular job sequence and move in orderly steps through the consecutive tasks.

The inability to provide extensive practice in individual tasks or combinations of tasks before moving along will remain with us as a serious disadvantage. Nevertheless, we shall have taken a step toward making effective use of the limited learning opportunities permitted by the often unalterable demands of the manufacturing process itself. Where operations cannot be maneuvered in a practical or economic way to establish good conditions or schedules for learning, as is often the case in on-the-job training, our response should not be to throw up our hands in despair but instead to adopt whatever useful training procedures can be fitted to the situation.

In summary, the indicated approach is to teach in parts that are within the grasp of the individual trainee. The problem of establishing connections later can be solved to large extent by providing the trainee with the sort of coaching which will focus his attention on the transitional signals which serve to carry him from one part to the next.

ASSIGNMENT

This assignment and the discussion cases which follow address themselves to the problem of determining the appropriate teaching units with regard to the nature of the job or to the trainee or both.

In many machine operating jobs, there are such separate tasks as feeding material into the machine, removing finished stock from the machine, making adjustments to the machine, repairing malfunctions and restarting the machine, cleaning or lubricating certain parts of the machine, etc. These tasks occur at separate times (are not continuous functions flowing one into the other without an interval of time) and are "natural" tasks for training purposes. But a further decision needs to be made in regard to each of the separate tasks: Is the task itself a good unit for learning or should it be broken down into sub-tasks?

Assignment: Break down one of your jobs into training units, applying the guidelines discussed.

CASES FOR DISCUSSION

Case 1

In a sewing machine operating job the trainee was taught to hem along an edge of cloth and to sew in a label at a specified location along the hem. She practiced the hemming and the label sewing in combination. The supervisor noted that she was fumbling with the labels as she tried to extract them one at a time when she needed them. The labels were stacked in a pasteboard container affixed to an upright part of the machine above and to the left of the needle. The container was open at the bottom except for a lip at the sides to keep the stack from falling out. The method of removing the labels from the container was to slide the individual label from the bottom of the stack by moving it forward ("tickling" it forward) toward the operator with the forefinger of the left hand and then grasping the emerging end with the forefinger and thumb of the left hand as the label moved forward from under the stack. The fumbling with the labels interfered not only with the sewing of the label but with the completion of the hemming. Performance in these phases of the task was ragged.

Question: What steps would you take to assist the trainee now? What approach (in terms of the amount to be practiced) would you have taken at the beginning?

Case 2

A supervisor was heard expressing the following complaint to another supervisor: "I've got this new girl on one of my assembly jobs. I don't know where the employment office is picking up these people. I placed this girl on one of my simplest jobs, putting five parts together, just five, mind you. They fit together in slots for the most part, except for two screws she has to insert and use a screw driver to tighten. That's all there is to it. And I gave her all the instruction anyone could ask for—had an instructor stay with her for a couple of hours.

"You know, she's still messing things up after two whole days on the job. Putting some parts in backwards or forcing them in without proper alignment. And boy, is she an expert with a screw driver! Wow! I'll be lucky if she hasn't punctured all of her fingers by the end of the week.

"The way we teach this job is to show her and tell her and let her practice, under an instructor, in the whole thing. It's simple enough. The people we used to hire had no trouble at all picking it up this way. But not this one. I could sure use some advice."

Question: What advice would you give this supervisor? What special problems may you encounter in breaking a job into training units for naive employees who may never have learned an industrial job before or employees who learn slowly?

Case 3

This is how another supervisor describes a problem he is having with a trainee: "You just have to restrain some people. One of my two new trainees, for example. We started him at the same time as the other one, and we've had to horse-collar him to keep him in line, to keep him marching along with the other. He's always wanting to run ahead, to tackle more of the job than a trainee should. Not that he's a poor learner; he just wants to decide for himself what size of bite he should take.

"Now, there's got to be some order in a training program. Once you set up a schedule of what to teach, you can have efficiency in your training only if you stick to that schedule. It's a system. It's like a time study or a quality testing procedure. You have to hew right to the line. You can't let a fresh kid right off the street tell you what to do or decide what he's going to do—a thing like this second trainee is trying to pull off, like I said.

"I know what the average trainee can take and that's the dose this fellow will have to accept. We just can't change the system for every Tom, Dick, and Harry who comes along."

Question: Do you agree with the supervisor? Is a training plan a system? Should there be changes for Tom, Dick, and Harry?

Case 4

A supervisor stated that the training program neglected to teach certain important parts of one of his jobs and explained how he went about remedying the oversight.

"On my machine operating job a man has got to move around. He performs a number of tasks at each machine, but he goes from one end of the machine to the other and he moves between machines. Sure, he's got to know what to do when he gets there—to the places where the tasks are to be performed. But it's just as important for him to learn how to get there, how to move fast from one place to the other. That's the travel element of the job, and he's got to be trained in it just like he's trained in feeding the machine, removing finished pieces, and the other parts of the job. Boy, he's really got to move.

"So this is what I do. I have him move from one end of the machine to the other, just back and forth not doing anything else, and I time him to bring him up to a piece-work pace. And I do the same about the travel between machines. I time him until he makes it over and over again. Of course, he already knows how to walk. But I'm training him to walk at the pace required to run this job. This is an element of the job he needs training in just like any other. After all, if you can time it, it's a part of the job you need to train a man to do."

Question: Do you agree with this supervisor? Do you consider this "travel element" a separate task for training purposes?

Case 5

A supervisor of a dyeing operation was describing to another supervisor a discussion he had had with a training man.

"I know it's hard for a new operator to learn how to run the dye job. There's a devil of a lot to learn. But I can't break up that operation, stopping it here and there along the way, just to make it easier for the trainee. You can't chop this job up. That's what I told this fellow. How impractical can you get!

"Imagine what problems I would have. You know how that job runs. You make up the dye lot; send a batch of material through on a very tight schedule—the stuff stays in there for just so long, you know, and then on to the drying unit for just so long. Am I supposed to make up six or seven dye lots just for make-believe, just for the purpose of training this new man? Or run the material back and forth through the dye bath and then back and forth through the drying unit? Tie up all that equipment, waste chemicals by the barrels, and ruin all that material? As I say, how impractical can you get!

"No, the only way to teach a new man is to let him pick up the whole operation by experience. Let him watch the whole thing until he's ready to tackle it. Otherwise he'll mess things up royally.

"I'm all in favor of training, you understand. But, unfortunately, I'm running a dyeing operation instead of a school for dye operators. My operation is different; that's all there is to it. The fancy ideas don't apply here."

Question: Considering the nature of this supervisor's operation, what practical advice would you give him in regard to the training of his operators? What training tasks do you see in this job? How should they be taught?

Chapter 4

How Long to Practice a Task

How long and how often should a trainee practice a job task? Four hours each day for two days? An hour each day for eight days? Fifteen minutes each day for 32 days? Or what? In drawing up a training schedule, this is the essential question which follows the determination of the tasks or units to be taught. Like the decision concerning training tasks, this decision also is somewhat dependent on the nature of what is to be learned and the sort of person who is doing the learning.

If the task to be learned is difficult or complex or long or not very meaningful and if retention over a long period is a major objective, the better approach is to distribute the practice rather than giving it in prolonged and unbroken periods. For simple, short, and meaningful tasks, the advantage seems to lie with massed practice, that is, staying at it for long, unrelieved periods. Massed practice also has its usefulness if we have delayed to the point where we have no other choice and need to retain what is learned for only a short time (until the test tomorrow morning, for example.)

There are exceptions to this general conclusion which associates massed practice with simple tasks and distributed practice with complex tasks. In tasks requiring the development of insight or the solution to problems (characteristics which may, among many, serve to make a task "complex"), some degree of massing may be helpful. For example, if the trainee is on the verge of "getting it" at the time a scheduled practice period is about to end, it would be foolish to take him from the task at that point.

Of course, the learner himself is a factor, since what is difficult for one may be relatively easy for another. Massed practice tends to pay off better with an apt and experienced learner, whereas distributed practice seems to have better results with less talented learners.

In general, the weight of the advantages appears to favor some degree of distribution. Much of the experience with the spacing of practice points to the beneficial effects of non-practice periods, which apparently permit the "settling" of what has been learned and the relief of physical fatigue, boredom, and frustration. Retention is also aided.

What goes on during the nonpractice periods will exert a major influence on retention. If forgetting or loss of skill occurs in the interim between practice sessions, the advantages of spacing are washed out. Such forgetting is most likely to occur if the interim is long and if interfering activities—such as the learning of other, particularly similar, tasks—are engaged in. The objective is to so schedule the practice in a task as to realize the benefits of spacing and to minimize the loss of skill through interference. One solution is to give relatively short rest periods between practice periods in a job task and to see that a minimum of interfering activities occur in the rest periods by attempting to enforce inactivity during the rest. The interim periods can apparently be lengthened without danger of appreciable loss of skill at a later stage of learning, when the new habits have become firmly established.

The total aim of the scheduling of training tasks can be boiled down to this firm establishment of skill. In terms of retention and the avoidance of interference, the arrangements which will assure "overlearning" are highly useful. The most practical arrangement of this kind appears to be a series of practice periods in each task interspersed with short rest periods (of a few minutes each) between practice periods. That is, the trainee is kept at the particular task until it is thoroughly learned and is given frequent rest periods to allow for "settling" and the recovery from fatigue and frustration.

If the job consists of a number of training tasks, interference and loss of skill are invited when the trainee is shuffled about from one task to another after just a few practice cycles in each. Instead, we should keep him at a single task, using rest periods to split up the practice, until overlearning occurs. His retention is better assured this way.

Of course, if the job consists of a number of tasks, the trainee must sooner or later move from one task to another. As a further measure against interference with responses already developed, it is advisable to schedule the tasks so that similar tasks (which interfere most, as we have discussed) are not practiced in adjoining periods. Such a schedule takes on even more importance when certain unfavorable occurrences (such as extreme boredom or loss of interest and motivation) force us to shift the trainee prematurely from one task to another. In such case the scheduling itself, since overlearning has not occurred, may be our strongest shield against interference.

In summary, our scheduling arrangements should:

1. Give the trainee enough practice in each task to bring about relatively "unshakable" skill and provide for rest periods between his practice periods in the particular task.

In a vestibule training facility, there are few practical problems to complicate the establishment of a desirable practice schedule. No production demands are placed on the vestibule equipment or machinery, and repetition of specific job tasks or subtasks can be arranged for any length of time without regard to the full job routine or perhaps even to the processing cycle of the machine. Within the mechanical limitations imposed by the machine itself (in regard to the stages at which we can stop it and backtrack for purpose of repeating the operator's tasks), we have the freedom to give the trainee practice in those units of the job and for those periods of time which make the most sense from a learning viewpoint.

Practice periods of a length and job tasks of a size most conducive to early learning are admittedly more difficult to arrange when training is given in the production department. When first-quality production is scheduled from a machine, downtime or unskilled operation for any purpose is costly. The question to be resolved by the supervisor is an economic one: To what extent can he interfere with the productive use of the machinery for the purpose of providing practice for the trainee? Considering that the long-run inefficiency of a learner is likely to result in a greater total amount of machine downtime and production loss unless he acquires skill quickly, the supervisor may be well advised to sacrifice a tolerable amount of production at the beginning. At least he should weigh short-term against long-term losses in production. And he should realize that the learning of multi-task jobs in the regular production routine, when that routine does not provide repetition in individual tasks, will encounter problems of interference and poor retention, will necessitate repeated promptings, and will develop slowly.

2. When it is time to shift to another task, move him to a task as dissimilar as possible (within the limits of available choice, of course) from the task he has just practiced.

The objective of such scheduling, as we have noted, is to keep interference at a minimum. A related question often arises: If the job tasks differ in difficulty, which should we start with? The evidence seems to show more facilitation from a difficult to an easy task than from an easy task to a difficult one. Such an indication would suggest the wisdom of scheduling the more difficult task first. This procedure could serve as a general guide, but it has limitations relating to the degree of difficulty the task presents to the individual trainee. If a task is so difficult (assuming it cannot reasonably be broken down into easier parts) as to prevent a substantial degree of success or movement toward success early in the game, the burden on the trainee's motivation may prove too heavy. It does not pay, obviously, to start with a difficult task if the trainee is thereby unlikely to stick around to reap the benefits of facilitation on the easier tasks. In a multi-task job, starting with a task of moderate difficulty, but one in which success can occur fairly soon, appears to be a practical solution to this phase of the scheduling problem.

CASES FOR DISCUSSION

The application of the principles involved in the scheduling and spacing of practice can be discussed with reference to the following cases.

Case 1

One supervisor gave the following explanation of his training schedule: "I observe people pretty closely. You've got to be a student of psychology to be a supervisor, you know. And one thing I've learned is that the new employees get bored with things in a hurry. Nothing interests them very long. That's a fact, and it's something you've got to base your training arrangements on. What you've got to do on the jobs in my department is to teach one thing at a time but not to spend too much time on each thing. Ten or 15 minutes is enough because if you stay at it any longer the trainee will just lose interest, and he can't learn if he loses interest. So it's 10 minutes on this task and 10 minutes on the next and 10 minutes on the next—my jobs have a lot of parts to them—until I get the whole way around. Then I may make another round. That keeps them interested, and that's why I think they learn better this way."

Question: What do you think of this approach? Is a fear of loss of interest a sufficient basis for this training schedule? What other factors need to be considered in setting up the training schedule?

Case 2

Of his schedule for training machine operators, another supervisor said: "Training arrangements have to make sense. That's my basis for setting up training schedules for my machine operators, for deciding what order they are going to learn the operations in. A reasonable basis, that's what it takes. Just common, ordinary horse sense. For example, these machines can be set up and operated to do a number of things, like cutting, chipping, planing, and so on. These operations are all different but some of them are more alike than others, if you know what I mean. They group themselves, you know, by being similar. And that's how I teach them. If these operations—the set-ups and how to run the machine—are similar, I block them off together and teach them in the same way, together or one right after the other because they resemble each other even if they're not exactly alike. That's the logical grouping of the job tasks and therefore the best way to teach them."

Question: Is this approach likely to result in early learning? In long retention? What advantages do you see, in terms of learning, in teaching by this supervisor's logical order? What disadvantages?

Case 3

A supervisor made this statement to a training man: "It's all very well for you to talk about giving a trainee a lot of practice on each part of his job, but it's just not practical in my department. We don't have any vestibule equipment we can rig up any amount of practice we want on. All we have to train on is the production machinery on the

floor. And I mean production machinery with emphasis on the word
"production." For example, if we teach a trainee to start and stop the
machines by practice on the production machines themselves—and I
admit there's a trick to it that requires a lot of practice to catch on to—
why, we just lose that much production. The starting part is OK but
let's face it, the stopping part is not. No, the only way open to us is to
let the new man try to learn each part of the job as the tasks occur in
the regular routine of the job. Some of these things don't come up
very often, but that's too bad. It's the only economical way to train.
Catch each thing as it happens, then on to the next thing. The trainee
gets plenty of practice that way."

Question: Do you agree with the supervisor in this case? If you
were the training man, what reply would you make? From a training
point of view, what disadvantages do you see in the foreman's "only
way"?

Case 4

A trainee was practicing an exacting task on a production machine in the department under the guidance of an instructor. After
every 15 minutes of practice she was given a break of a few minutes.
The instructor noticed that the trainee was nowhere to be seen during
these rest periods. During the fourth rest period when the trainee dis-
appeared again, the instructor went looking for her. She found her at
a machine in a remote corner of the department, frantically trying to
perform the task she was supposed to be resting from. When the instructor approached her, she said, "I was sure you wouldn't mind. In
stead of sitting around, I thought I'd just try to learn this thing."

Question: If you were the instructor in this case, what reply would
you make to the trainee in regard to the usefulness of breaks?

Case 5

A frustrated supervisor explained his difficulties to his superior:
"The answer to my problem is to cross-train my operators so that
when we change styles or change the production schedule up or down
on our various items, I can shift experienced operators into the
breach. I know this is the answer, but I can't seem to make it work out.
When we go to peak production on one item or other and I move operators to a different machine—machines they've been trained to run
at the beginning—to meet the demand, well, we just drop dead. My
efficiency goes to pot, I don't get the expected output, and my schedule flies out the window.

"I don't understand it because every time I hire a new operator I train him on all four machines in this department. I go through the whole bit, machine by machine. On the first one I explain, I demonstrate, and I let him run through a couple of cycles until he gets it. Then to the next machine for the same treatment. And the third. And the fourth.

"All of my people have been through this kind of training. They all know how to do it. Why can't they perform when I really need them?"

Question: What answer would you give to this supervisor? How can "cross-training" be done so as to take hold?

Case 6

"Some trainees act just like willful children," a supervisor was heard to say. "This new girl, for example. My instructor is having trouble with her. Over nothing at all, really.

"We have a schedule set up for teaching the job. A good one, too. So much time to be spent on the first job task, so much on the second, etc. And we give breaks every so often to keep the trainees from getting tired or bored. It's all lined up—a certain time for practice, then a break, more practice for a certain time, then another break, more practice, another break, and so on. It's great. Just like clockwork.

"But this new girl apparently can't be scheduled. One time she asked the instructor if he would mind if she took a break early; she told him she guessed she was tired before she was supposed to be. And one other time, when she was struggling with the toughest task of them all, she said she didn't want the break right then, said she just had to try for a breakthrough, as she called it, and couldn't afford to be interrupted just then. She sulked like a child when the instructor insisted that she take a break.

"I guess she just doesn't understand the purpose of the breaks."

Question: How would you handle this trainee? What would you tell her about the purpose of the breaks? Who does not understand the purpose of the breaks? The foreman? The employee? Explain your answer.

Chapter 5

The Equipment and Job Methods for Practice

Since we are not engaged in training for training's sake but to provide an employee with skills needed in running an actual job, the question of transfer of training needs to be answered as we set up our training arrangements. How best can we assure that what is learned during the training period will apply to the job?

An obvious answer is to get as close to the actual job as possible, to duplicate it if possible through the teaching of actual job methods and procedures and through teaching these methods with the actual machinery, equipment, tools, and materials of the job. In certain cases, hazards and excessive costs would prohibit this arrangement. But if we therefore resign ourselves to teaching an approximation of the job, we must recognize that the skills developed in training will not fully transfer to the job and to some extent may interfere with the final development of job skills.

Equipment and Machinery for Training Purposes

Transfer difficulties are invited in vestibule training establishments which use outmoded machinery and equipment differing in terms of operational principles and operator methods from the machinery and equipment on the production floor, or which use material of a type requiring somewhat different handling than the regular stock. As discussed earlier, under the right conditions we can expect transfer of identical elements and common principles. But the differences will get the trainee into trouble, and explicit training arrangements need to be established to increase the probability that transferable skills will actually transfer and, when assignment to the job is made, that the new elements and principles are learned.

Transferring of Elements

If we consider as a transferable element the pattern of motions and perceptual feedback needed to perform a job task or subtask, we can feel confident about its application to the job if the job requires the same pattern. The trouble arises when segments of the pattern have to be changed—when the trainee's responses have to be altered, or when the sequence of responses is changed, or when the feedback signals telling the trainee where he stands are different or missing so that he cannot pick up the information on the effect of his acts on the work in progress or is picking up the wrong information. In such a case, new links have to be forged in the chain or the old links shifted from one position to another.

To leave it to the trainee to rebuild the chain is to ask for trouble. His usual tendency is to rely on what he has learned in training, to assume a greater transfer than is possible, and to fail in a number of trials before he begins the painful process of patching his method. That process will be slow because the old responses tend to persist, getting in the way of the new. In addition, the trainee is often in a poor position to determine on his own what specifically needs to be learned or how to go about learning it. In short, he needs guidance—and insightful guidance, because the business of rebuilding a chain of responses and related signals is not simple. Practice in extremely small segments without a link-up with surrounding segments of the motion pattern may be, for example, a wasteful procedure. The teaching units need to be designated for the trainee, and the trainee needs to be given adequate coaching in relearning the task.

Transferring of Principles

In regard to principles, it should be recognized that a principle is not learned until the trainee can apply it.[1] If we train on vestibule machines which are somewhat different from the production machines but may involve the same principle of opera-

---

[1]See Robert M. Gagne, THE CONDITIONS OF LEARNING (New York: Holt, Rinehart and Winston, 1965), pp. 141–171, 231–235, for discussion of the learning of principles and the conditions of transfer.

tion or mechanical construction, we may assume that the principle is learned. To induce the trainee to take the appropriate steps under instruction in the vestibule is not sufficient evidence of such learning.

For example, let us say that in the vestibule a repairman or operator had to set up a machine so that, on each cycle, a subassembly is positioned at a certain height and that the raising of the subassembly is accomplished by means of a lever system. Let us assume further that the production machine uses a lever system for this purpose but that the arrangement of the levers is different (levers in different positions, different location of fulcrums, and different lengths of arms). In both instances—in the vestibule and on the job—let us say that the subassembly is affixed to one end of a lever and the power is exerted on the other end of the lever. The arm transmitting the power is attached to the lever by means of a stud and slot. The operator controls the height of the subassembly by positioning the stud in the slot.

It would be an easy matter in the vestibule period to teach the operator a simple procedure applying to the vestibule machine by providing him with a little self-prompting statement to memorize: "right to raise, left to lower." He will then move the stud to the right in the slot to raise the position of the subassembly (if it is too low) and to the left in the slot to lower it (if it is too high).

He has learned nothing in this instance about the principle of leverage, nothing about the relationship between the lengths of the resistance and effort arms of the lever and the amount of vertical movement at the end of these arms. If he knew the principle he would understand that moving the stud to the right had the effect of shortening the effort arm in relation to the resistance arm (supporting the subassembly) and, for that reason, caused the end of the resistance arm to move up a greater distance. And conversely, he would understand that moving the stud to the left in the effort arm increased the length of the effort arm, and for that reason the same vertical movement exerted on it would move the resistance arm (with the subassembly) a lesser distance than before.

But to adjust the height of the subassembly on the vestibule machine, he need know nothing of this. The need arises when he attempts to set up a machine on the production floor and is faced with a different arrangement of levers. At this point he is likely to (1) apply the old rule of thumb and find out it will not work (meanwhile causing considerable loss of time and probably also damage to machine and stock) and (2) resort then to trial and error to develop a new rule of thumb (which will take even more time and may result in even greater damage).

Similarly, if an employee is expected to replace gears to increase or decrease the speed of rotation of a shaft, he can be taught to follow a procedure or he can be taught the principle involved—or both. A procedure may be enough for satisfactory performance on the vestibule machine; such procedure might include (1) the reading of a table or the memorizing of a rule of thumb to settle upon the proper size of the "change" gear for the desired speed of shaft rotation and (2) the steps required to replace the gear. If, however, the gear train on the production machine is somewhat different and the old table does not apply and no new one is provided, the trainee is ill prepared to come up with the size of gear which will give him the specified speed. He may be able to put one on but which one? How many teeth should it have? He cannot say because he has not learned the principle underlying changes of speed through gears— that the rotational speed of the driven gear is determined by the ratio of the number of teeth in the driver gear to the number of teeth in the driven gear.

If we expect the trainee to rely on principles to assist him in facing the job demands, we had better teach him the principles. And we cannot be assured that he has learned—this is the crucial point—until he does apply them correctly in differing situations. Consequently, our training should be carried beyond the point at which he demonstrates a knowledge of the principle by application to a single situation (as, for example, applying it to one vestibule machine); he should be presented with the opportunities to apply it in a number of situations. These may be rigged situations not always involving the presence of the actual machinery. Whatever the arrangement, the objective is to provide training in the transfer of the principle to new and varying situations, so that when he goes on the job he will be prepared to apply it there.

Individual differences are a factor in the learning of principles. Some trainees tend to generalize their knowledge much better than others, seeing in new situations the similarities and relationships which suggest the applicability of learned principles. This difference indicates the need for a varying amount of practice from individual to individual in the learning of principles. The rewards of genuine learning are considerable since, once learned, principles are not easily forgotten.

The concentration on the teaching of principles and the emphasis on identical elements in the training period do not, however, relieve us of the responsibility for assisting the trainee, at the time of assignment to the actual job, in effecting the transfer of whatever skills are transferable and in learning what is newly required to run the job. For example, the employee who really learns a principle on a vestibule machine will understand what has to be done in a certain situation on a similar production machine; but he needs to be taught the precise pattern of motions required to do it efficiently.

We are particularly vulnerable to transfer problems when an experienced employee is hired into a department with previous job training over which we have no control. He may come to us with different methods and with an understanding of different principles; and his application of these products of earlier learning may lead to inefficiency, waste, damage, and frustration. A thorough check-out of an experienced operator's skill and knowledge is needed in order to limit the attempted transfer of skills to the usable ones and to provide for the teaching of whatever remains to be learned for performance of the job in the way we want it done.

These problems with outside learning are troublesome enough; we would be foolish indeed to create transfer problems of our own by training inexperienced employees in operations, methods, principles, and the like which lack any significant amount of direct utility on the job. In this regard, we must be wary of small differences between training and production in respect to machinery and materials; these can prove to be disturbingly interfering. One manufacturer, finding that its sewing machine operators were thrown off stride when moved from the vestibule machine to a machine on the line (same make and model), cleared up the problem by permitting the trainees to take their training machines with them into production. The "feel" of these supposedly identical machines was different. In hosiery looping, a slight change in the denier of the yarn as the trainees moved from training status to production caused a definite downturn in indices of progress. The "different feel" of the new hose, involving stretch and other small distinctions, necessitated a period of relearning.

Job Methods for Training Purposes

Training on the job itself eliminates a great many sources of transfer problems since the machinery and materials used in learning are the actual machinery and materials of the job. Even so, we may still get into trouble. The transfer problem in this case resides in the job methods since it is just as possible to teach erroneous methods in a production department as in a training room. If we allow the trainee to use whatever methods are easiest for him, despite their inefficiencies, we are often faced with a staggering task of retraining when it is time to move him to expected levels of output, particularly if we have allowed these supposedly temporary habits to be strongly built. The skills developed in performing the job in the wrong way do not transfer to performance by the right method and in many cases will severely interfere with the learning of the right method. This is not to say that a trainee can immediately begin to use the approved methods; some shaping of the trainee's responses is necessary to bring him to that method. But the objective, if we are to minimize the transfer difficulties, is to get as close to the method as we can at the beginning and to move to it as swiftly as we can.

Because of the greater possibilities of interference, the learning difficulties are increased in jobs which require a shift from one style of product to another, each requiring a somewhat different (although similar) sort of handling. Perhaps the most effective training approach in such a job is to keep the trainee on each style long enough to bring about overlearning to combat the effects of retroactive interference (between styles) and increase the employee's chances of retaining what he has learned.

The control over job methods in our training efforts begins with the definition of the job. The instructor has to know in exact detail what he is to teach, that is, the correct signals and motion patterns. With this definition or description of the job as his "textbook," he is in a better position to cover all of the aspects of the job and to prevent the trainee from coming up with incorrect or inefficient habits or from missing certain key points that are crucial to performance. Because of his very skill, the instructor himself must be made newly aware of the details of the job methods so that he can teach, in a conscious way, even those aspects of the job which he performs automatically—the key points he "takes for granted" because they are now so imbedded in habit. Another advantage of a definition of job tasks is that it helps assure that each trainee will learn to perform the job in the same efficient way, thus contributing to the general efficiency of operation within the department.

Kind of Job Description Needed for Training

A strict methods statement of the type used in industrial engineering (stressing operator motion patterns) is a helpful start but does not go far enough for training purposes. It is particularly deficient in the perceptual aspects of the task. Since the job definition must be translated through training into knowledge and skill on the part of the trainee, it should take a form useful for that purpose and specifically designed for that purpose. Job definitions to be used in training should include several types of statements in order to provide the instructor with what he needs in order to impart the necessary skill and knowledge to the trainee. A useful framework for the construction of such a definition is given below.

     1. Knowledge items (aside from those relating to job method). These are the items which the instructor will explain to the trainee. They include:

        1.1 The usual location of things.

        1.2 The meanings of terms peculiar to the job or special terms used in teaching it.

1.3 The mechanical features of the equipment or machinery. (In detail appropriate to the job. Obviously, an operator needs to know less than a repairman.)

1.4 Safety hazards, quality requirements, housekeeping, waste standards, information on supplies and supply usage.

1.5 Standard (or required) times for performing a task, machine cycle time, schedules (cleaning, lubricating, patrolling, etc.), and priorities.

2. Statement of the motion pattern. This statement is the source of the instructor's priming of the trainee through explanation and demonstration and his cueing of the trainee in early practice. It includes:

2.1 The sequence of motions in the task.

2.2 What motions are involved (reaches, moves, grasps, etc.)

2.3 What hand and finger positions are required in making the motions.

3. Perceptual feedback items. These are the items which the trainee must pick up (first with the help of the instructor and later on his own) as indications that something needs to be done and that the doing is progressing well or poorly. They include:

3.1 The signal to begin a particular task—that is, the evidence that something needs to be done by the employee. A discrimination is required here. The trainee must learn which conditions or situations require him to perform step A as distinct from step B, B instead of C, etc.

3.2 The way things should be if the task is performed in the right way. These items might be considered standards of performance internal to the task and standards applying to the end product of the task. They include the required positions, distances, amounts, tolerances, tensions, appearance features, etc.

3.3 The reference points or attention points the trainee can use to find out whether he is achieving the
required positions, distances, tolerances, and so
forth as he runs through the task and completes it.

3.4 The sensory channel he should use to find out.
Should he look, listen, feel, or what?

The later discussion of instructor techniques will illustrate
how the instructor uses explanation, demonstration, cueing,
and feedback to teach the job to the trainee. At this point we are
simply saying:

1. In order to teach a job efficiently, we must define it first,
even if we teach it right on the production floor. We need to
know exactly what to teach. Otherwise we may saddle ourselves
with retraining problems complicated by interference from
well-established but poor habits fostered by our own lack of
specificity.

2. If we are going to use the definition to teach by, the
closer the definition fits the instructional techniques the more
useful is the definition.

CASES FOR DISCUSSION

In the cases that follow, the transfer of learning is the foremost
consideration. In discussing these cases, the supervisors should arrive
at conclusions concerning (1) what factors in the situation or in the
training arrangements are causing difficulties of transfer and (2) how
the transfer can be maximized.

Case 1

A repairman trained on old model machines was placed on new
high-speed machines. Some of the mechanical principles used in the
old machines were also used in the new. But the old friction clutch
was replaced by a different type of clutch assembly; the braking action
was caused by the pressure of internal expansion against the drum
rather than external contraction; the lever system used to raise the
feed table to aligned position for processing was replaced by a screw
thread; and the mechanical motion which served to stop the machine
when malfunctions occurred was replaced by an electronic system.

When asked if he could repair the new machines, the repairman replied, "Machines are machines. I've been on those old ones for 10 years. I practically rebuilt them, and I can handle these new ones."

Question: Could the supervisor expect the employee to repair the new machines without trouble? What training help, if any, should the repairman receive?

Case 2

A supervisor hired a new girl to go on a packing job. The method of the job was to pack two items at the same time, putting each in a separate small cardboard box. But since the items were fragile, he decided to start her out by having her pack one item at a time, using her right hand (she was right handed) to move the item from the supply bin and position it in the packing box. He cautioned her about the care required in the handling of the items, citing the cost to the company if the items were broken in the packing process. The girl was pleased to start out this way because she had always considered herself to be awkward with her left hand.

The supervisor, after instructing her on the first day, came back to her on the fourth day with the intent of moving her into the regular two-at-a-time method of packing.

"Now that you know how to do it," he told her, "We'll just do it the same with both hands. There's nothing to it. Just do it the same way but use the other hand, too."

Question: Did the trainee really know "how to do it"? What difficulties do you see in shifting her to the two-handed method? What would be the reason for difficulties? How would you have trained this employee?

Case 3

A supervisor in an assembling department was having quality problems which he found were associated primarily with one assembly station. At this position the employee operated two small presses to attach two parts, added another part by inserting it into a slotted recess, and screwed in another part with a small powered screw driver. The sequence was as follows:

Step 1. Insert part 1 by operating a press.

Step 2. Insert part 2 by positioning it into a slot by hand.

Step 3. Insert part 3 by operating a second press.

Step 4. Insert part 4 by operating a powered screw driver.

The problem with quality was centered chiefly in the first two parts. These parts were occasionally defective to begin with, and the positioning of these parts by the operator was a critical matter since even a slight misalignment would cause a malfunctioning of the entire unit.

To solve his problem the supervisor inserted an inspecting task into the sequence of operations, scheduling it as step 3 right after part 2 had been inserted. The assemblers were told about the new inspecting operation and were given training in it. The training consisted of explanations and illustrations of the various defects found in parts 1 and 2 and explanations and illustrations of the proper alignment of these parts and the possible misalignments. Then the operators were told to return to the job and see that they performed this inspection function after step 2 of the old sequence, combining it at that point with all the old steps in the sequence.

At the end of the next week the supervisor reviewed his quality records and found that the percentage of defective units had not gone down; in fact, it had gone up a little.

Question: Why, do you think, no improvement occurred? What is your opinion of the training arrangements? How would you have retrained the assemblers?

Case 4

A new man was hired as an operator of a delicate machine used for precise shaping of small parts designed for electronic equipment. When he reported for work, he made the following statement in a conversation with his supervisor: "I've operated a lot of different machines in my time, from bulldozers on down, and I've learned two rules. The first is that if you're having troubles with the machine, just increase the power and let 'er rip. Nothing works perfect, and you can overcome little difficulties just by overpowering them. Besides, it's production that counts so you've got to keep the machine going. The second rule is that if something doesn't work and everything else fails, just give the thing a kick or jar it with your hand. Sometimes things get stuck or haven't settled exactly right, so a good sharp blow will set things to right. That's what my experience on machines has taught me. I don't see that there's anything different about machines from one place to the other. It's the nature of the beast. They can be ornery if you don't know how to handle them."

Question: What problems do you see in training this man for the new job if he tried to apply his "rules"? How would you go about training him?

Case 5

A supervisor described his difficulties with a new inspector in this way: "You know, we process material sent to us by other companies and ship it back to them. One customer accounts for half of our production and the other two split the rest. Of course, the way the work comes through, we shift from one customer's work to another at pretty short intervals. It's got to be scheduled this way. Having these three customers means that we follow the inspection standards they specify, and these standards are different in regard to what defects can be accepted in first quality goods, what defects are considered repairable, etc. Our biggest customer has the strictest standards.

"The best way I knew to train the new inspector at the start was to teach her the standards we use for our biggest customer. That stands to reason because she would be looking at their stuff more than the others. I thought I'd cover the standards to use for the other two companies as she had occasion in the regular course of the job and the regular flow of the goods to inspect their goods. That's what I did.

"Boy, what a mess! That girl can't keep anything straight. Everyone is howling. Not only is she fouling up these smaller customers, but I'm catching the devil from our biggest customer. It seems like this girl has been putting a lot of their goods into first quality which shouldn't be there because of the defects. She should know what they will accept; I've gone over that with her thoroughly. She's too loose with them and too strict with the others. As I say, what a mess!"

Question: What is the reason for the mess? How would you regard the supervisor's training arrangements for teaching the differing standards? Would you have gone about it differently? How?

Case 6

A supervisor expressed the following complaint about the performance of his sewing machine operators: "You know, I took this methods course some weeks ago, and I came up with a prize idea on my sewing operation. The way we've been sewing blankets in my department for years has been to sew binding on one end of the blanket, using a binding machine, and to overedge the other end, using an overedger, of course. But with two operators, one to do the binding and the other to take the blanket from her and do the overedging. Now, here was my brilliant idea: to put an overedging machine and a binding machine at the same workplace and to have the same operator perform both operations—that is, to do the whole job on the blanket instead of messing around moving the blanket from one sewing table to another. I worked out the design of a table on which I could mount both machines within easy reach for the operator. And I was ready to go.

"I gave these operators every opportunity to learn the combined operation. I trained them until the cows came home, even though most of them had had experience on both machines before. These machines are somewhat different but they are both sewing machines, so I didn't expect any trouble. But I didn't take any chances. I trained.

"But do you know, not one of them has been able to make the piece-rate on this combined operation. Not a single one. But, by heavens, they'll come around to it or they'll get out. This idea is too good to be fouled up by a bunch of stubborn operators. I could cut my sewing costs 20 percent with it."

Question: What, do you think, might be the reason for the failure of the operators to produce on the new operation? What advice would you give the foreman at this point? From a learning point of view, what are the problems in shifting between machines?

Case 7

A supervisor hit upon what he considered a "revolutionary" approach to training. Here's how he described it:

"I've got a training system for my assemblers that really makes sense. These girls have to put some very small parts together, and so they've really got to develop skill in using their fingers. So I teach them to use their fingers first. I have them practice using their fingers on a pegboard. You know, putting small pegs or pins in holes drilled in a board. It stands to reason that the knack of handling the small pegs will really help them when they start assembling parts. You see, what you do first is to train them in a certain ability—like handling small things—and then they can use that ability wherever it's required. Pegs or parts, it makes no difference. That's the secret of training."

Question: Does the "system" really make sense as a training approach? Are there any difficulties in this approach which you would call to this supervisor's attention? How would you train assemblers? Can you train employees in "how to handle small things"? Consider the matter of transfer to the specific job tasks.

Part 3

TECHNIQUES OF INSTRUCTION

Introduction

We are now confronted with the trainee. We have settled on our training arrangements; we have decided upon our teaching units, our schedule for instruction, our job methods, our training equipment and materials. What happens now?

An instructor or supervisor has a number of choices. Explain the task and turn it over to the trainee? Explain and demonstrate and then turn it over? Walk off at this point? Stay and observe? Haul out the stop watch? Coach the trainee during practice?

Even when he selects his teaching techniques or combinations of techniques, there are the additional questions of the form of the technique, the amount to be used, the length of time to use it, and (as it is used) its effectiveness with the individual trainee. Although we have fewer answers than questions, the answers or partial answers are still numerous enough to guide an instructor in the productive use of instructional techniques.

The instructional techniques are discussed at length in the next three chapters. Before such discussion begins, however, attention should be called to the underlying importance of the trainee's preparation for learning. Unless he is ready or can be made ready, the instructional techniques are likely to make very little imprint on him. His preparation is largely a matter of motivation (which is discussed in its broader applications later in the text), and right at the beginning of his training period the instructor may be able to "open" him to learning by such steps as:

1. Introducing him broadly to fellow workers and assisting him in breaking the social ice.
2. Taking as many of the uncertainties out of his situation as possible by giving him information on aspects of the job, training arrangements, and the many other topics which may puzzle a new employee.

3. Making his training as meaningful as possible. This step might include:
   - Showing the trainee what part his job plays in the manufacture of the product.
   - If the job is divided into parts for training purposes, explaining what is accomplished in each part and how the parts will fit together to make up the total job.
   - Defining the terms, peculiar to the job, which will be used in training him.
4. Most important of all, maintaining and showing an attitude of confidence in the trainee's ability to learn the job and a manner reflecting sympathetic understanding and patience.

In summary, we need to reduce the pressures on the trainee, hasten his adjustment to the work environment, put "sense" in the training we have in store for him, and expect success from him. Efficient learning will then not automatically follow, but the groundwork will have been laid for it.

Right at the beginning the instructor should do a quick bit of learning himself. He must "learn his man" in a hurry so that he can shape his approach (1) to the learning experience the individual trainee brings to the job and (2) to the trainee's own progress. It is essential that the instructor accurately size up the amount of prompting (given by his instructional techniques) the individual trainee will require.

Chapter 6

Explanation

Explanation in job training is primarily used to convey information (and bring about understanding and retention) concerning two main topics: job requirements and job methods.

The information on job requirements is concerned with the "surrounding" aspects of the job. These items of information deal with hazards at the workplace, quality standards, efficiency requirements, housekeeping, supply usage, waste standards, etc.

The amount of information given at one time and the timing of the explanation will have strong influence on retention. If the trainee is given more information than he can remember, he may himself select what is important for him to hold onto—a selection which is often poorly based on naive ideas of the job. The position of the items in the list is also a factor; the items in the middle are the least likely to be remembered. In regard to timing, quality requirements make little impression on a trainee at the stage when he is struggling to master the elementary hand skills of the job. Nor does the giving of information on the expected piece-rate level of output make much sense at this early stage. Information on these goals should be fed to the trainee when he needs it and has some hope of attaining the level.

The wise course, therefore, is to avoid overwhelming the trainee with information. Instead, give it to him in amounts he can absorb, and schedule it in terms of his needs. One ground rule: Safety information always comes first.

Whatever is to be told to the trainee—at whatever time— should be organized for presentation, preferably in the form of checklists or written notes. A reliance on memory for coverage of safety points, for example, is likely to leave some major hazards unmentioned. There should, of course, be order in the data to begin with (top to bottom, left to right, for example, in regard to physical hazards on a machine), and there should be order in the presentation itself. A checklist, no matter how logically constructed, will serve little purpose if the supervisor or instructor hops in random fashion from item to item as he gives his explanation to the trainee. In such case the trainee must organize the scattered material himself, a task he is not prepared to tackle at this point. If the items are of varying importance, the supervisor should clearly indicate the differences by using more repetition with the important items, by giving them special emphasis, by getting back to them at the end, and by centering most of the questions on them.

Of course, the presentation should follow common-sense rules of communication, aimed at increasing the trainee's opportunity to learn. The supervisor should:

• *Take it slow.* Put the trainee at ease and give him undivided attention. Speed does not allow for the "sinking in" of the message, and interruptions chop up the presentation so that the learning dividends of our organized presentation are minimized.

• *Repeat.* Do not assume that the trainee has the message with one exposure. The part played by repetition in learning and retention cannot be overstated. The "must" items particularly need the benefit of repetition, both during the course of the presentation and in the final summing-up.

• *Use words the trainee understands.* Otherwise he will give his own meaning to what he hears and may misunderstand. The meaningfulness of the information is dependent on words— and learning and retention depend to some extent on meaningfulness. So on various counts, the words themselves must make sense. In addition, the functions or objectives themselves, expressed through the words, should make sense to the trainee. We tend to assume that quality, efficiency, safety, waste control, and housekeeping are self-evident goals which need merely to be stated in order to be accepted and applied by the new employee. Unfortunately, these objectives may not have the same absolute and imperative value for the trainee as they have for the supervisor. At the least, the explanation should make clear to the trainee economic and other consequences to the company—and to the employee himself—of failure to meet the standards and expectations attached to operational goals.

• *Use sketches or visual aids or a view of actual equipment or machinery* in order to get to the trainee through more than one sense if the material lends itself to more than one approach.

Perhaps most importantly, an adequate effort should be made to assure that the trainee has understood or, at least for the short term, remembers what was told to him. The supervisor should therefore ask questions and have the trainee play back the information to him. The form of the question is important. It is often useless to ask, "Do you understand?" The invariable answer is "yes" whether the trainee understands or not. The best question is a specific one, asking for a recitation of facts.

The best question also is one introduced along the way. A common fault in explanation is to wait until the end before asking any questions of the employee. So much may then be found unclear as to require a complete replay. A final set of questions is advisable in order to sum up where we stand, to fill in gaps at the end, and to reestablish the relative importance of items. But these last chores are made much easier if questions on specific points are raised along the way, at the time when the specific points are explained. The playback should be a continuing technique as well as a summarizing technique.

In summary, the explanation should have at least the following features if understanding and retention are our objectives.

1. Have material organized in advance.
2. Give an orderly presentation. Cover items in logical order. Place emphasis on most important items.
3. Give the trainee a chance to learn. (Go slow; use repetition; make the points meaningful; appeal to more than one sense if practical.)
4. Assure that trainee has understood. Use questions. Have trainee play back the information. Use an overview to fill in whatever gaps remain.

The second major purpose of explanation is to give information to the trainee concerning job methods (the hand and finger positions, moves, reaches, sequence of steps, etc.)

Timing is an important consideration. Explanation of job method "after the fact" is of limited use. Explanations should be given before the employee practices the task—accompanying the demonstration, advisedly—or as he is practicing it. Preferably, explanation should be provided at both times. Explanations will be needed later in the correction of errors, of course; but to reserve the bulk of the methods explanation until practice has progressed some distance is to put an extremely heavy burden on the corrective efforts. Errors are likely to be maximized because the trainee will not have had a beginning explanation to prompt him. In addition, the delayed explanation may lose the value of immediacy; the employee may find it difficult to tie the comments retroactively to his specific acts.

The value of the beginning explanation (and demonstration) lies in providing insights helpful to a productive practice. We shall have to clear up errors, of course, in any event; explanations are needed all along the way. But there is little point in inviting errors by starting our explanations late. The objective is to minimize the trainee's errors at the start and then to zero in on specific errors (rather than trying to clear up a general mess) with our later explanations and other techniques.

In explaining the job method, the instructor should stress the key moves (those affecting efficiency, quality, waste, and so forth) and the reasons for those specific points of method—that is, why the task must be performed with these particular moves and in this particular sequence and the consequences of erroneous methods. In addition—and equally important—he should point out the signs which tell the trainee that he is performing the task in the right way. As they show up in job performance, job methods are not simply a number of discrete responses but are a series of moves interspersed with perceptions of results. Knowledge of what to perceive and how to perceive it is as essential to the trainee's learning as a knowledge of the moves to make.

Telling "why" is a recommended practice not only to assure efficiency and the attainment of other operational objectives such as quality, waste control, and safety but also to facilitate the learning of method. If the explanation relates the method to the operational goals, the method then makes "more sense" to the trainee. The "why" adds meaning to the information; and the more meaningful the thing learned, the faster it is likely to be learned and the longer retained.

Since quality, efficiency, waste control, and safety are basically the product of job performance, they should be built into the job method and taught in such a way as to become an habitual part of the employee's regular job routine. Of course, he should know the standards and objectives relating to these performance results; we have discussed the sort of explanation useful for this purpose earlier in this chapter. But the means of meeting the standards should be taught as aspects of the job skills the trainee develops through practice—in a process which begins with explanations and demonstrations.

ROLE PLAYING AND DISCUSSION

The exercises and situations that follow are intended to give the supervisor practice in terms (1) of handling explanatory material, (2) of coping with the varying problems of communication represented by individual differences among listeners, and (3) of placing explanation in proper perspective as a means of teaching job skills.

Role-Playing Exercises Involving Explanation

1. Present information on safety to a new employee going on one of your jobs.

2. Present information on quality requirements to a new employee going on one of your jobs.

(Note: These should be situations of simple information-giving. The supervisors should practice giving information by using role-playing. Their performances can be judged on the basis of the pointers for effective explanations presented earlier.)

Situations for Discussion (or Role Playing)

What particular difficulties might you encounter in giving information on safety or quality to the following new employees? What explanatory pointers from those suggested in this chapter would be most useful? How would you handle the explanations?

I'm Jane Crompton and I've never worked in a factory before. In fact, I've never worked anywhere before except on my father's farm. I'm willing to work and I'm anxious to learn about this job, but I get so nervous when the supervisors are around. I've always had the reputation of being shy. I get flustered when someone in authority talks to me. I had that trouble in school. And when I was interviewed for this job I was shaking all over, just like being in the principal's office.

*   *   *   *   *

I'm John Hendricks and I've been around. The way I look at a new job is this: I listen politely to what they tell me—some of it is just plain bull—and then I do it my own way. That's how I made out on other jobs. I didn't hold them long, I admit, but I've never been on relief. No sir.

*   *   *   *   *

I'm Henry Hutchens. One thing I've learned in the last job is that you can't trust a supervisor. That last fellow was a dishonest slob; he couldn't tell a straight story if it killed him. I got so I just didn't listen to what he said. It just went in one ear and out the other.

*   *   *   *   *

I'm Jerry Smithers. I was valedictorian of my class, and if I do say so, I knew more than most of the teachers. I find it's the same way with supervisors. I've had two jobs before this one and I've found out that I can tell exactly what the supervisor is going to say before he says it. And what they say I already know anyway. There's no point in listening to them. They're a bunch of dumb clucks.

*   *   *   *   *

I'm Ted Balser. I've always had trouble in school. I have trouble remembering. And on the job it's the same thing. If they give me enough time, I'll catch on. But the supervisors usually don't take enough time. They tell you to do something once and that's it. What I usually do is go to one of the other fellows to find out what the supervisor meant. But if the others don't know, I'm sunk. Like when I turned out the wrong-size pieces on my machine in my last job. They fired me for that, but I just hadn't got the dimensions straight.

Statements for Discussion

Here are several statements made by supervisors concerning the use of explanations in training. Do you agree or disagree? Why?

Here's what I do. I take the methods statement and have the trainee study it, have him more or less memorize it. In detail. This really cuts down the training effort we have to make with the new man. We can almost eliminate the demonstration and the helping hand when he starts practicing the task. He's already on his way. He knows how to do the thing.

*   *   *   *   *

I tell 'em the expected piece-rate output right at the start. So there's no mystery about it. They're entitled to know what we expect of them. So then they know, right at the beginning. Besides, it's a sort of test. If they don't feel they can make it or don't want to give the effort, it's better that they get out. It's better that we settle it right off.

*   *   *   *   *

Information confuses the trainee early in the game. He's not ready to absorb it. So I hold off. I let him get a good start. Then I clear up the information on job requirements and the job method. My motto is to let 'em learn "to do it" first and learn "about it" later.

Chapter 7

Demonstration

Demonstration gives a picture or model of the task being taught. It teaches what is to be done and gives a picture of "how," but it does not teach the "how" alone. The trainee learns how to perform a task primarily by doing. Once the demonstration has been repeated enough to give the model, the trainee should begin to practice performing the task. There is little reason to force a trainee to spend hours watching the instructor or another operator run the job. Unless the task is complex and cannot be broken into easier parts, several demonstrations (along with explanations) are usually enough as a starting prompt.

As with explanation, common-sense pointers can serve within limits as useful guides in giving demonstrations. Obviously, the trainee should see the demonstration clearly. If the motions can be slowed down without giving a false picture of the job method, they should be. If necessary to preserve the method, the speed of motions should be maintained; but the number of demonstrations will have to be increased. If the process itself does not permit the slowing down of the instructor's motions, he should repeat the demonstrations at the required speed until the picture is clear. The trainee should face in the same direction as the instructor so as not to confuse the right and left hands. The trainee should hear the instructor distinctly if explanations accompany the demonstration, as they should.

However, there is more than the strictly obvious in the procedures to be followed in giving a demonstration and in the purposes behind demonstrations. An expanded procedure involves a walk-through of the demonstration using cues and feedback—that is, giving short statements or explanations concerning the motions (what and how) as they occur and identifying the signs that give knowledge of results and guide the operator through the task. In this way the words are associated with the action, and the trainee is prepared to make meaningful use of them as they are fed to him later in his own practice cycles.

Demonstration without clarifying explanation tends at times to result in mere mummery. The view of a task being performed may give the trainee an idea of the motion pattern but may fail to make clear what specifically is accomplished by the particular motions, or precisely how the accomplishment comes to be, or what the evidences of the accomplishment are, or how the trainee is to detect the evidences. For example, the demonstration of the task of feeding cloth into an attachment on a sewing machine shows that the hand is held in certain positions and that the fingers make repeated rolling or turning motions. But to copy this motion pattern will result in very little unless the trainee realizes the purposes of the hand positions and finger motions and is given reference points by which to tell whether that purpose is being served.

To provide the trainee with reference points in the demonstration is difficult for the instructor if his own perceptual feedback is given by the kinesthetic sense, as is often the case with highly skilled employees in the performance of certain tasks. The instructor cannot use his "feels" as points of reference because they are not something he can share with the neophyte trainee or communicate to him. In addition, they are inappropriate in the early stages of the trainee's learning; at this point the trainee is normally and necessarily dependent upon visual or auditory signals (usually visual) as his sources of reference. For this reason the instructor must roll back his own experience and supply the trainee with such visual signs as he used earlier and as are needed currently by the trainee in the development of intermediate levels of skill. Beginning with his early demonstrations and accompanying explanations, he must instruct the trainee in what to look for as he progresses through the task. At a later stage, as we will discuss in Chapter 9, he will attempt to shift the trainee to a reliance on "feel."

There is merit in finding out if the message of the demonstration has gotten through to the trainee. To be sure the trainee has a picture of the task being demonstrated, it is a good idea to have the trainee march the instructor through the task, telling him what steps to take, the key points in the motion pattern, and the main signals of success. If the trainee shows that he has a good picture of the task, the time for practice has arrived.

A word of caution is in order concerning such playback from the trainee. It can be easily overdone and can indicate an erroneous or exaggerated notion of the function of the early demonstration. A perfect statement by the trainee of the fine points of performance is not required at this stage. Recitation is not an act of motor skill; learning how to recite a task is not equivalent to learning how to perform it. If the sequence of steps and the principal items of method and feedback are known by the trainee, practice should begin. Demonstration, however skillfully done, does not replace practice; it is a preparation for it.

If skillfully done, a beginning demonstration will help keep down the number of performance errors; but it can hardly be expected to eliminate them. A good prompt, as indicated earlier, is a good start in the training process. If we use our prompts effectively, there is less trial-and-error learning and less confusion to clear up when the trainee gets into the act. But the demonstration is only a start.

Fruitful and repeated use of demonstrations should occur as the learning progresses and should be directed at a diminishing number of specific errors. If a task is complex, re-demonstration of the entire task may be required after the trainee has begun practicing; even with the best of prompts there are sometimes too many errors to permit a concentration on specific weaknesses. With repeated prompts as a preparation for practice efforts and adequate coaching during practice, the trainee will usually reduce his errors quickly to the dimensions we can cope with by direct attacks on separate faults.

It should be borne in mind that the faults, as skill develops, are less likely to lie with the motor aspects of performance than with the perceptual aspects. The later demonstrations should tend, therefore, to focus more sharply on the trainee's use of feedback—on the attention points he relies on as he works through the task, on the information he picks up at such points, and on his interpretation of the information. It should help him to so shape his acts as to achieve, in a smooth and rhythmic pattern of motions, those exact positions, distances, tolerances, and other aspects of precise and refined performance that genuine skill demands. Skilled performance is something much more than the mimicking of a demonstrated series of motions.

Since the linking-up of segments of a task is so essential to improvement, before completing his particular set of corrective demonstrations the demonstrator should cover those elements adjoining the precise point of error as well as the error itself. The demonstrations can concentrate on the specific error at the start but should move, with satisfactory explanation, to the larger pattern of motions which adjoin and include the element in which the weakness exists. Corrective efforts which deal exclusively with isolated and somewhat meaningless fragments of the task are likely to bring mimimum results.

The Use of Audio-Visual Aids for the Purpose of Demonstration

The above discussion would suggest that audio-visual aids can serve a useful purpose as a means of demonstrating but that they may tend to become less useful as the trainee moves from a lower level of skill to a higher.

In the very early stages of learning, as the shaping process gets underway, we are primarily concerned with prompting the trainee so that he can run through the task in the right sequence of steps, using an approximation of the method. At this point, motion itself as well as the terminal positions and results of the moves is an important aspect of the model given by demonstration. In addition, the trainee at the beginning needs to take a look at the performance of the full task. In view, then, of our modest early objectives and the beginning needs of the trainee, a silent motion-picture or televised representation of the method is useful—not adequate in itself since explanations of purpose and key points of method are required, but useful. With accompanying sound which itself gives the clarifying explanation, the film or TV tape takes on increased value.

At a later stage, when we are not so much concerned with

moves or responses as with perceptual feedback, the use of audio-visual devices must be fitted to the trainee's shifting needs. To assume blindly that a repeated look at the filmed method will somehow clear up all the errors and bring about a refinement of method is a foolish expectation based on an erroneous idea of how skill develops. If a trainee is still having problems with gross moves—making too many or making them in the wrong sequence, for example—then another look at the film would help. But, as indicated earlier, the mere copying of a motion pattern does not add up to an act of skill. Fairly early the trainee needs to build into his performance a series of quick perceptions of how things are progressing. The moves themselves become less important to his learning than the means of interpreting where he stands with each move or at the terminal point of the move so that he can proceed through the task in a discriminating way, making the moves that work out, being aware that they are working out, and bridging them quickly and smoothly.

To be helpful in this regard the film or TV tape must pause now and again to indicate clearly the points of attention for visual feedback and the signs that should appear at those points as a signal that all is well. A series of slides showing the key attention points, with accompanying explanation and with superimposed legends specifying the distances, positions, tolerances, and other exact dimensions of the visual indications, may be appropriate at this point in training.

The problem is more complex when the feedback is simultaneously auditory and visual or a mixture of the two occurring at different times in the task. Audio-visual devices may be of some help in such cases if both sensory media are well handled. But the difficulties increase. If the feedback or part of it is tactile, audio-visual devices are of very limited use. They can show contact, but the usual audio-visual devices cannot communicate to the trainee the lightness or firmness to the touch, the amount of pressure, and so forth.

We may find, moreover, that these aids are futile when the trainee develops to the stage when he needs to shift to a dependence on kinesthetic feedback. Films and sound obviously cannot reveal the kinesthetic aspects of performance. The skilled operator demonstrating the task on film is "feeling" his way through the operation with his muscle sense, but only the visible part of the performance is revealed to the watching trainee. The crucial perceptions are hidden; they cannot be communicated to the trainee strictly by film or other pictorial representation, even when such representation is augmented by sound.

Much has been made of the potential value of television in job-skills training, particularly in regard to the opportunity it affords for quickly playing back the trainee's visible performance to him. When combined on a tape with the pictures of the approved method, the employee's method then stands revealed to him as matching up or not, and a close scrutiny will further disclose the specific moves that are in error. Again, however, we are faced with the troublesome fact that a matching of motion patterns is not a matching of skill. The trainee must do more than revise his wayward motions when a discrepancy occurs; the perceptual requirements must be taken into account. Even those motions which appear, in the comparison with the "standard," to be correct may be considerably less effective in terms of actual accomplishment than the "same" motions of the skilled operator shown on the TV tape.

This is not to suggest that audio-visual devices do not usefully serve in the prompting and correcting of a trainee. The point is that the trainee needs much more help than they alone provide. And if they are to give additional help, they must somehow contrive to focus on the perceptual aspects of performance as well as on the response pattern.

Use of feedback is a crucial and difficult aspect of skill development. The cyberneticists especially are to be commended for their ingenious efforts to construct feedback devices.

Meanwhile, here stands our old friend, the instructor. It would be ironic to dismiss him before we learned how to use him effectively. In one vital phase of instructing, the direct coaching of the trainee during early practice, we have not always realized that he could serve a function. It is to this phase of training and to this function of the instructor that we will turn our attention in the next chapter.

STATEMENTS FOR DISCUSSION

The case material which follows presents various points of view concerning demonstration. In discussion of this material, the supervisor can sort out the good and poor uses of demonstration and so come to conclusions concerning the proper function of demonstration in the learning process, the effective means of performing it, the importance of the perceptual aspect of the demonstrated performance, and the importance of fitting the demonstration to the specific need of the trainee at his particular stage of learning.

Here are some statements from supervisors on how to train new employees. Do you agree or disagree? Why?

1. Here's the way it's done. I tell them and I show them and then I leave it up to them. Of course, I check back now and again to see how they're doing. But the main way they learn is by paying close attention to me when I show them.

2. People don't learn very well if you mollycoddle them. For example, taking them by the hand and showing them over and over how to do things. If they really want to learn, once is enough. And if they don't want to learn, well, this will prove it.

3. I've got a man to put them with—one of my best operators—to show them how the job should be done. Of course, he doesn't let them get in the way. And he's a quiet kind of fellow—doesn't say much to anyone and least of all to a trainee. But they learn a lot from just watching him. He really can run his job.

4. You've got to start them slow. The way I do it is to put a new man alongside one of my old operators for a full day. Just to watch him. That's what I tell the new man: "Just watch and you'll really learn how it's done." That's all. And I don't push them. I give them a whole day or maybe even two days of watching. Then they're ready.

5. I have a sure-fire way to tell if the demonstration has "taken." I have the trainee run me through the operation. I mean in detail, telling me exactly what I should do at each step and why. The fine points, too. Now this may take a long time, but then I know he's ready. After this, I can pretty much forget about him. I can just tell him, "Now you can do it, so go ahead."

6. The best way to demonstrate is to show the trainee the wrong way, the errors he should avoid. I get that set in his mind. The right way will take care of itself once he knows what to avoid. He can figure it out pretty much on his own.

7. I've got a film on this assembly job of mine that is so good that

even a child can follow it and know exactly how to perform the job. The close-ups are tremendous; they get right down to every little motion, every little position. Every little flick of the finger is right out there for everyone to see. No commentary is needed. I just put the trainee in the room by himself and let him run the film loop continuously for several cycles. Then I take him out to the job. His instruction is just about complete at this point.

8. You can't overplay the demonstration. I've got a good film for demonstrating the proper job method, and the way I use it is to show it to the trainee every morning for the first several weeks. Right on the dot at 7 o'clock each morning. That way, the trainee knows exactly what to work on the rest of the day.

Case

Two supervisors were discussing the difficulties they encountered in teaching the "fine points" of highly skilled jobs to trainees.

First supervisor: "It stands to reason that if a trainee can look at and study the right method, he can pick up the fine points of the job. I've got this trainee right at the verge of running the job at the piecerate pace and giving me a really skilled performance. It has been a struggle, let me tell you; but he's almost there. Just needs to pick up the refinements, add a little precision and speed, and he'd have it.

"And it's all there, all the fine points he needs, right there in the film. And he's got eyes to see them. So I've been showing him the methods film. Again and again. But he just hasn't picked up what he needs. I don't know why. It's all there in the film. You'd have to be blind to miss it.

"You know what that fellow asked me? He said, 'What am I looking for?' When it was all there right in front of him! How blind can you get!"

Second supervisor: "I know what you're up against. I have a man at about the same stage, almost there but not quite. And I thought I had the answer. I put my most highly skilled operator with him, not only to show him but to sort of diagnose his troubles, you know, put a finger on the little things that seem to be holding him up.

"Well, this old operator stayed with him for a little while and then came back to me and told me that the trainee was just taking too long finding out if he was right on one move before going to the next, that he seemed to be hung up or to hesitate here and there along the way. 'A kind of a loose and jerky bundle,' that was how he described the trainee's performance.

"Well, I thought we had the game won at that point. I told the old boy to just get back there and tell the trainee how he could find out whether his moves were working or not. Guess what he told me? He said, 'I can't do it. I don't know what to say to him.'

"That was a silly answer, I thought, so I put the question to him: 'Well, how do you check to tell whether your own moves work out or not. I mean you yourself. How do you do it?'

"His answer just about floored me. Remember now, he's my most highly skilled man. The real expert. 'It's not a matter of checking exactly,' he said. 'I just know I'm right. I just know it somehow.'

"He just knows it! Maybe a little bird told him. That's a lot of help to the trainee."

Question: What advice would you give to each of these supervisors? What sort of help do you think is missing in these instances, help of a sort which would lift the trainees over the hump? What should accompany the demonstration? What is the reason for the skilled operator's difficulties in instructing the trainee?

Chapter 8

Direct Coaching

The instructor's work does not stop after his explanation and demonstration. He should not stand back and merely observe as the trainee attempts to perform the task. The practice is not a "test" to see what the trainee has learned from explanation and demonstration. The practice is crucial to learning, the most essential ingredient in the development of skill in the performance of the job tasks. The instructor should have a direct hand in the learning process at the point when the practice begins. He should perform two main functions: *cue the trainee and provide feedback to him*.

The Use of Cueing

The instructor should cue the trainee by telling him, in short phrases, exactly what he is to do (and how to do it) as he comes to it. The idea is to lead him through the operation or job task, cueing him in advance of each part of the cycle, to increase the chance of early success in performance. The cueing is intended to bring the trainee quickly to the point where he can go through the task on his own. The cues therefore should be cut out when no longer needed. In order to know what cues can be dropped, what cues need to be retained, or what new cues need to be introduced, the instructor at certain intervals should run the trainee through the task without cues. He will usually find that the trainee can readily perform some parts of the task but will have continuing difficulties with others. On those parts where the help of cues is still needed, cues should be used. Finally, when the successive test cycles, after intervening series of diminishing cues, show that the trainee can repeatedly perform the task correctly without the help of any cues, all remaining cues should be dropped.

Often the trainee will move ahead of the cues to perform certain parts of the task correctly. In such case the instructor is informed, without the use of a test cycle, that certain cues can be discontinued. He must be alert, however, to mistakes caused by the trainee's premature efforts to plunge ahead without help; in such instance he should restrain the trainee. It is useful at the very start of the practice to direct the trainee to respond to the cues rather than to make largely exploratory motions. If some measure of success occurs, the instructor should recognize it; but the instructor's function is to provide the guidance needed to elicit correct responses at this point. Usually cues can be dropped rather quickly, but it is too early to do it during the first cycle or two.

It should be kept in mind that doing is not always the same as learning. The intent of the cueing is to induce the trainee to perform the desired act, but his performance of the act may not represent learning. He has learned only when he can perform the act without being prompted.[1] The assumption is that the cues will get him into the "swing" of making a series of responses and that this pattern of responses, through repetition and reinforcement, will be sufficiently established to stay with him. But we cannot be sure of this development until we see him perform the act on his own. Cueing, therefore, should be adequate to prepare him to go on his own but should not be continued beyond the point of need. As stated, the cues should be phased out when the trainee is sufficiently primed.

Instructors tend to operate at extremes in cueing a trainee. If an instructor continues this prompting too long, he may set up a habit of dependency; that is, the trainee may learn primarily to respond to the instructor's cues and may at the end be unable to perform the act, except for certain segments, when the instructor withdraws. This difficulty is most likely to occur when the act is complex or involved. The other extreme is to allow the trainee to proceed by trial and error, an arrangement which puts a premium on the accomplishment of the task but

---

[1]See B. F. Skinner, The Technology of Teaching (New York: Appleton-Century-Crofts, 1968), pp. 206–219, for a discussion of priming the learner's response and freeing the response from the prime.

puts little value on method. Learning may occur by this procedure, but it is often the learning of an inefficient motion pattern and thus results in inefficient performance. In addition,
the extent of the learning is often questionable since the accomplishment of the task may not be associated with the means of
accomplishment. That is, the trainee finally achieves the purpose of the task but may be slow to identify the particular steps
(of the innumerable ones he took as he muddled through)
which had the effect of moving him forward.

So much for trial-and-error learning. It's a luxury industry
can ill afford. This statement is made in spite of experimental
evidence that retention may be better if the trainee develops his
own insights. The insights, if related to "successful" completion
of the task—simply finishing it off—may result in the learning
of inefficient methods. The trainee may learn, that is, to complete a task by the wrong route. In addition, the time required
by the trainee to develop his own insights may be so long as to
generate problems of motivation and excessive training costs.

The better approach is to give the trainee the sort of help,
including cueing, which will move him quickly through the
proper sequence of steps and through the right method at each
step and to withdraw the help when we are assured, through
his unaided performance, that he can perform a task alone,
that the objective of retention can be realized. Such assurance,
however, requires that he satisfactorily perform an act repeatedly, that he is on his way to "overlearning" and has not just
lumbered through the task in a seemingly acceptable way, perhaps by accident, once or twice.

In teaching complex tasks, the instructor should change
cues at various stages of learning so as to shape the trainee's motions progressively and bring them along to the desired method. For example: First use cues referring to the steps to be tak-
en and the sequence of steps. Then use cues to bring about the
correct hand and finger positions and the specific motions for
the various steps. Finally, use cues to teach the fine points of the
task (exact positions, distances, tolerances, etc.)

If the task to be taught is a simple one, the process of lead-
ing the trainee by stages to the desired method is not required

to the same extent. The exact method can be taught or closely approached, with cueing as a principal technique, at the very beginning.

The Use of Feedback

The instructor should feed back information to the trainee, telling him he is right or wrong and, if wrong, giving specific information on the nature of his error.

A trainee needs to know if he is right or wrong. Since he cannot determine this for himself at the beginning, the instructor should provide the information by telling him or signalling him in some way. There is a tendency among instructors to tell a trainee when he is wrong but to say nothing to him when he is right. It is important to his learning of a task that he know when he is right. Knowing he is right is a reinforcing, that is, a rewarding, experience for him and helps assure that he will do things in the same way again when the situation occurs again. It increases the probability that he will repeat the response when the situation recurs.

If he is wrong, it is not enough to tell him or signal him simply that he is in error. He needs to understand the exact nature of the error so that he can be in a position to try to correct it. He needs to know the size, the direction, and other characteristics of the error. And he needs the earliest opportunity (with further explanation, demonstration, and practice in the correct method under coaching—cueing and feedback) to perform the task correctly.

To be effective, feedback must be immediate and specific. This is not to say that the instructor must feed back information concerning every motion the trainee makes. But he cannot allow too many motions to go by without providing feedback. That is, the instructor should provide information to the trainee at numerous times while he is working through a task and again when the task is completed.

The feedback should be directed at what is being taught. If the instructor is concentrating on the procedure (without attention to precise method), then the instructor should feed back information only on the trainee's performance in working through the steps. If method at each step of the task is being taught, the feedback should tell the trainee if his reaches, moves, hand and finger positions, and the like are right or wrong and, if wrong, in what respect.

Cueing and feedback should be used in conjunction with one another. They also should be used insightfully, in terms of the general purposes served by these coaching techniques and of the needs of the trainee as learning evolves. At the very beginning of practice, an instructor finds he must concentrate largely on cueing because at such an early point he must be concerned primarily with eliciting responses. As practice continues he is less involved with cueing and increasingly occupied with the feedback needed to reinforce the correct responses he has brought forward and to modify and shape the incorrect or approximate responses.

Feedback is especially important in refining the trainee's performance; it provides information on how he stands or is progressing at various checkpoints along the way. These checkpoints are the perceptual and often measurable points in the trainee's travel through the task; they have to do with, among other things, exact positions, lengths, distances, tolerances, turns, tensions, amounts, quality indications, and appearance.

If the feedback informs the trainee that he is right, it triggers the next move or series of motions in the task. If it informs the trainee of error, it is a signal and guide for making an adjustment or correction.

As stated previously, the feedback is given early in the learning process by the instructor, whose purpose, however, is to provide the trainee as quickly as possible with the means of checking out his progress. If the instructor looks at certain signs for feedback information, he should shift the burden of checking for those signs to the trainee. At first he is the trainee's eyes and ears; soon he has the trainee using his own senses at the various checkpoints within the task and the final checkpoint at the end of the task.

As skill develops, the feedback becomes more and more a matter of feel and less and less a matter of seeing. The skilled operator has the "feel" of his job; the feel (primarily from muscles involved in movements) tells him how he is coming along.

The instructor should attempt as early as possible, once the method (involving motion pattern and visual feedback) is mastered, to force a reliance on feel as a means of feedback in those parts of the task where the skilled operators rely on feel. Of course, in those tasks or subtasks in which vision continues necessarily to provide the feedback and is the most efficient channel for feedback, the trainee should be taught to continue to rely on it.

Schedule of Feedback

The best schedule of feedback will depend upon the trainee's stage of learning. As the trainee is picking up the method, feedback should be used consistently. Once he is able to perform the task correctly and the training problem is to keep him performing it that way, the feedback should be given only now and again. In addition, the form of feedback can change since errors have been eliminated; the feedback will become advisedly praise and recognition of the trainee for being right. But it should never be dropped altogether by the instructor, even at the very end of the training period. Used now and again late in that period, it is perhaps our best assurance, aside from actual follow-up observations, that the trainee will take the taught method into the job itself when he goes on his own.

From Feedback Devices to a Reliance on the Trainee

One of the most promising and challenging applications of training devices and display arrangements is in the provision of feedback to trainees. The devices are useful when they give information quickly to the trainee as he works through the task. They are most useful if they can provide not only signals to the trainee that he is right or wrong but also information which will assist him in interpreting his error (its magnitude, direction, etc.) and thus prepare him to make the specific adjustments needed for correction or improvement of performance. It is in this latter respect that we need to improve our devices, and it is in this respect that an on-the-spot instructor has been found in most situations to be extremely helpful and, up to this point, virtually irreplaceable.

Whatever the source of feedback at the beginning, the ultimate need of the trainee is to rely on himself. If we lose sight of this objective we may teach him to rely on imposed feedback not inherent in the nature of the task itself and to develop intermediate habits which will slow his progress to higher levels of skill. For example, to use a stop (wooden block, for example) to teach a reach of a certain length may result in a reliance on the block if the device remains beyond its useful period of service. The aim is to have the trainee provide his own feedback—in the case of the reach, to have his "feel" take over ultimately as the sign that his reach is covering the proper distance.

STATEMENTS FOR DISCUSSION

By discussion of the following material, the supervisor can perhaps be helped to place the deserved emphasis on the instructional techniques of cueing and feedback which can be used to elicit, stamp in, and refine the trainee's responses. These are techniques which should be at the core of our training program and should command the most skillful efforts of the instructor instead of being ignored in an exclusive reliance on demonstration and explanation or weakly used as a supplement to these other techniques.

The following are statements by supervisors concerning various aspects of coaching. Do you agree or disagree? Why?

1. The only way to tell that someone has learned is to try him out. That's the way training ought to proceed. You prepare, you present—you know, explain, and go through the motions yourself. And then you use practice; that's the application step, to see how much he had learned. The presentation is the most important step. I'm a firm believer in the old saying: "If the learner hasn't learned, the teacher hasn't taught." This means he just hasn't presented it right. If he had, the trainee would be able to go right through it without help when it got to be time for application or tryout.

2. If you feed back information to a trainee, you ought to wait until the trainee completes the task he's working on. That's the way I do it. He goes through the whole thing. Then we discuss it.

3. You talk about learning what is right and wrong on a job. Well, experience is the only teacher for that. No one can really help you with that. You try one way and if it doesn't work, you try another way, and so on. It sticks with you better if you learn it that way.

4. I'm a firm believer in testing. That's the only way you really find out if someone has learned. I give the trainees a fair chance. I let'em go at it, but at the end of the week I check'em out thoroughly. I have them show me and tell me and then I give them another week to work on it. And so, week by week, I test them out until they can manage on their own.

5. Everyone knows a trainee gets nervous if he has someone hanging over his shoulder. I don't allow it. I understand how the trainee feels—he's nervous enough as it is—and so I don't permit it. You've got to let the trainee work things out by himself, to get over his nervousness by being alone at the beginning. He'll come along okay if you don't get him flustered right at the start with a lot of attention. When he gains more confidence, then you can work with him.

6. I have some ideas about what to tell a trainee. If he's right he knows he's right because what he does works out. If he's wrong he knows that, too, because what he does turns out bad. That's all there is to it. It's best not to tell him anything.

7. I don't agree with not telling a trainee how he's doing. You might skip telling him when he's right—he ought to know that—but you sure ought to tell him when he's wrong. I don't think, though, that you ought to confuse him with a lot of details when he's wrong. Knowing he's wrong ought to be enough to start him back on the track. After that, he's got to figure out some things for himself.

8. We usually bring in five or six trainees at a time and assign them to an instructor. It works out pretty well, I think. While the instructor works to start one of the trainees the others learn a lot by looking on. And so down the line. And after each of them gets started, she goes up and down the line to observe them and make corrections.

9. If I find one of my trainees using a poor method, I correct him right away. I explain and show him the right way and then I watch him go through it a number of times—don't disturb him at all. Then, if he needs it, I explain and demonstrate again. And I watch him again. And so on until he finally has it.

CASES FOR DISCUSSION

Case 1

An experienced employee was teaching a new man how to operate a machine. He gave him considerable practice in the tasks of feeding material into the machine and removing the finished product but
would not allow him to start or stop the machine—the most highly
skilled tasks of the job. The trainee complained to the supervisor.
When the supervisor asked the experienced operator whether he
had, in fact, refused to allow the trainee to practice starting and stopping the machine, he replied indignantly, "Of course, I wouldn't let
him do it. It's too ticklish. He'd just ruin the stock and mess up the
machine."

Question: What advice would you give the supervisor in this situation? How would you suggest the trainee be taught to start and stop
the machine without "ruining the stock and messing up the machine"?

Case 2

Two supervisors were debating the relative merits of cueing and
feedback.

First supervisor: "I'm all in favor of letting an employee know
how he's doing, especially if he's having trouble and making mistakes.
That's the main thing about instructing—straightening things out.
That's the main part of guiding a trainee. He's got to move into it on
his own, and then you shape and refine what he does by calling attention to errors."

Second supervisor: "I take a different tack. What the trainee
needs most of all at the beginning is to be steered through the task.
You tell him what to do as he is about to do it, that is, you cue him all
the way through with little prompts here and there. The rest will take
care of itself. He'll realize, on his own, when he's right or wrong, and
he'll go ahead and make the necessary adjustments."

First supervisor: "But he won't know what adjustments to make.
That's where the feedback really pays off, in clearing up the errors—
the wrong or inexact moves, the extra motions, and so on."

Second supervisor: "But if you had cued him in, he wouldn't
have so many errors to clear up with your feedback. He wouldn't
need it."

Questions: Whose position would you support in this debate? Would you take a position different from the two presented? If so, what is it and how would you defend it?

Case 3

A supervisor stated that his training consisted of treating the employee "like an adult." As he explained it: "The employee himself has got to decide what help he needs and when he needs it. When I start a new man, I emphasize the open door. I tell him that he is free to see me any time he has trouble. My door is always open.

"That's the way you should treat adults. You give them the opportunity to learn—hiring them into the job is really the opportunity. It's up to them to take advantage of it, so you make them responsible for it. That means starting them on the job without any fanfare—without surrounding them, or looking over their shoulder, or forcing your attention on them. You just provide the help they need by assuring them that you're available when they call. That's the main point, the key to training adults.

"This approach works. The proof is that they learn the jobs and hardly any of them bother me at all."

Question: What do you think of this supervisor's approach? Is this the way "an adult" should be handled? What do you think of the supervisor's "proof" that his approach works?

Part 4

LATE STAGES OF LEARNING

Introduction

Beyond learning how to perform the job tasks by the right method, the trainee must still learn:

- To run the job at the required speed. Speed is a crucial requirement in the learning of piece-rate jobs.
- To "organize" the job, that is, to learn how to use his time in such a way as to stay on top of the job. Organization is the "make-or-break" requirement in the learning of jobs involving a number of tasks and a number of machines.

The learning process, particularly at the late stages of learning, may involve periods of time when little or no progress is in evidence. These periods show up as plateaus in the learning curve. We discussed plateaus earlier, simply to point out that they occur. Our reason for discussing them now, when we have brought the trainee along to a point when plateaus tend to afflict him, is to decide what might be done about them.

As a reminder, here is what we are confronted with:

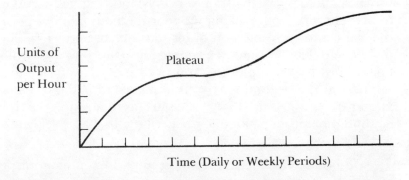

Time (Daily or Weekly Periods)

We will start this section of the manual with a few ideas about combating plateaus and then proceed to examine how speed may be acquired and job organization learned. As is clearly evident, these are interrelated items which bear directly upon the trainee's climb to an acceptable level of job skill.

Chapter 9

Moving Upward to Genuine Skill

What to Do About Plateaus

The so-called genuine plateaus that are necessary for development of skill and therefore unavoidable, are somewhat rare. In many cases, a leveling-off period has a cause which an instructor or supervisor can do something about.

1. The trainee's motivation may flag. He may become discouraged or lose interest in the job. *Suggested countermeasures:* Make sure the trainee is prepared to learn; teach him in such a way as to assure some measure of early success; let him know how he is doing; use feedback effectively; show a personal interest in him; display confidence in his ability to learn.

2. The trainee may be using poor job methods. Poor methods will limit the trainee's progress and require him to exert too great an effort. *Suggestions:* Teach the approved method from the start and observe the trainee closely and frequently enough to prevent him from picking up poor methods. Do not permit the trainee to use a method of his own invention or a method that "comes easy" to him. In simple jobs (short-cycle assembly operations, for example) the approved method can be taught virtually at the beginning. If it is impossible for the trainee to master the finished method at the start (as in sewing), the trainee should be pushed along to the final method as quickly as he is ready.

Do not permit the trainee to acquire a fixed habit of performing a job task by a method which should serve only as a temporary step on the way to the final method. For example, in sewing, the instructor may allow the trainee to stop the machine several times to position the cloth early in the training period. But the instructor should move the trainee to the right sewing method (continuous feeding of the cloth into the machine without stops for repositioning) without the sort of prolonged delay which will make a fixed habit of an inefficient method that we intended only as an intermediate stage in the process of shaping performance.

3. The trainee may have difficulty with a certain task or certain aspects of the job or at certain levels of skill development. Normally the trainee picks up the easy things first; he slows down when he tackles the more difficult aspects of the job. *Suggested countermeasures:* Undertake an analysis of the trainee's difficulties and do the necessary coaching to get him over the hump. The instructor should remember that not all trainees find difficulties in the same job aspects. Consequently, the kind of leveling-off relating to task difficulty will occur at different times for different trainees and will be of different duration for different trainees.

Often an employee experiences a plateau as he is in the process of making the transition from one level of skill to another. On objective indices of performance, for example, he may appear to be resting on dead center as he develops sensitivity in a new sensory channel for the purpose of perceptual feedback (most commonly, shifting from visual to kinesthetic feedback). Similarly, no visible signs of progress may show up on the indices as the trainee struggles to establish the skills of job organization which will enable him to tie together the separate task skills and assume control of the total job. Suggested steps which an instructor or supervisor might take to expedite the movement of the trainee from one level of skill to another are discussed later in this chapter.

4. The trainee may not be given adequate opportunity to learn. If a trainee is taken from his job to do other work (such as miscellaneous chores in the department), or if, within the job, he is shifted too quickly from one task to another, his progress will be slow. *Suggestions:* Set up and adhere to a training schedule which will provide sufficient practice and use adequate instructional techniques. In short, keep him at the tasks and coach him in performing them.

5. The trainee may encounter changes in material or equipment. Even small changes can throw the trainee off stride. *Suggested remedy:* Train the employee for what he will do on the job;

train him with the materials and equipment of the job. Don't shift him to something else during or after the training period. If a variety of materials has to be handled and a variety of machines has to be operated on the job, keep the trainee on one task (one type of material or one machine) long enough to make the learning stick. That is, have him overlearn the task before going to something else.

In summary, an instructor should be aware of leveling-off periods in the individual's progress (should have the progress data which will reveal such periods), should analyze the trainee's difficulties to see what can be done to help the trainee resume his progress, and should take the steps suggested by the analysis. If the plateau is actually a necessary part of the learning curve of the trainee on a particular job, the instructor should at least explain to the trainee that such leveling-off is normal and should encourage persistent effort until the upswing occurs.

Finally, the instructor should realize that plateaus, whatever their cause, are highly individual. They occur at different times for different people, and their lengths and frequencies will be different. The task of the instructor is to spot them whenever they occur and do something about them.

Acquiring Speed

Although there is some truth in it, it is too easy to say that we should build speed on method, that first we should teach the job method and then work on speed. The job method, from the learner's point of view, is more than a conglomeration of motions; it includes the required perceptions which must be integrated with the job motions and the means of bridging from one segment of the task to the next. If we work on these perceptions and bridges as part of our attack on job methods, we are, in effect, working on speed since they are a major source of skill improvement. They give the trainee a facility in proceeding through the task which will show up in a reduction in required time.

Reaches and moves, the methods elements which appear prominently in the usual statement of job methods, are not the parts that lend themselves to improvement in skill or speed. The "manipulations" at the ends of reaches and moves, such as positioning, grasping, and selecting, are apparently the major payload; and it is in the performance of these more precise and discriminatory elements that perception plays an essential role. It must be imbedded in the method if skill and speed are to develop.

We shall look at a number of means for increasing performance speed. Our intent at the outset is to indicate that the various aspects of acquiring job skill (including speed) are closely bound and that while we may give the appearance of building one part on another, there are concurrent and overlapping developments in the learning process itself which make our neat categorizing only partly valid.

At the least, we should get our terms straight. We should see the job method as a broader statement of what is to be learned than a motion pattern. If we are to build speed on any foundation, it must be the basic pattern and sequence of overt acts which make up the skeletal framework of the task. And if we must outline the progressive stages (allowing for overlap), we can say with some assurance that they probably deal with:

1. The basic motion pattern
2. The perceptual aspects
3. The refining of perception and the shifting of perception to different sensory channels
4. The bridging aspects involving anticipation—an aspect which is present in all the stages but probably has its greatest and more-or-less terminal development in the third stage.

It will be noted that the sort of evolution we ascribe to speed is basically the development of skill itself.

This outline, as general and tentative as it is, does not suggest the extent of the difficulties encountered in the development of skill and speed in the full job. One major source of difficulty is the unevenness with which skill evolves in the subparts of a single job task or in the various separate tasks of the job. In one subtask or task the trainee may reach a high level of skill (perhaps our third stage) but remain at an intermediate level (our second stage) in another. Our training approach must soon take the shape of diagnostic efforts aimed at specific and varying areas of difficulty.

Use of Perceptual Feedback

Once the trainee can perform the basic pattern of motions in an elementary way, the instructor's emphasis should be placed on those signals which tell the trainee how well he is doing at key stages of the cycle of the task. That is, the instructor should provide him with a way of knowing, on his own, whether he is achieving the exact position, distance, length, tension, tolerances, quality, turns, amount, appearance characteristics, and so forth as he proceeds through the task. As such a standard of performance is perceived as being met, it serves as the cue for the next motion or series of motions. Thus, the amount of hesitation is reduced as the trainee threads his way through the operation; he comes to know immediately that he is doing all right so far and may proceed. The perceptions not only serve to tie the task elements together but also sharpen the motions themselves.

The instructor must realize that there are limits to the speed with which the human senses pick up signals. If the signals are numerous and occur at the same time or at very short time intervals or if the eye must scan a wide area to pick up scattered signals, the trainee will need time to sort things out, to "process" the information before he goes on. The instructor can do nothing to increase the sensory speed itself, but he can direct the trainee to the signals and can help him interpret them, with the idea, as indicated earlier, of shifting this burden to the trainee.

Shifting to a Different Sensory Channel

As stated earlier, the further development of speed in many industrial tasks requires the trainee to move from a reliance on vision to a reliance on "feel" (through the kinesthetic sense) to get the signal that things are right or wrong. In this way the performance of the job becomes "automatic."

The building of a tight bond between response and feel

will take considerable ingenuity on the part of the instructor
and considerable time and effort on the part of the trainee.
And we may find that we can expedite the process in only a limited way by instructional techniques. But a knowledgeable attempt is in order. Sometimes the training in reliance on feel can
be arranged by cutting off the trainee's vision by some such device as having him look away from the contact point where his
hand or tool meets or affects the material. Such a procedure
eliminates the feedback provided to the trainee by his visual
perception of the effect of his acts upon the material being processed. The trainee may find it helpful if the instructor temporarily reintroduces himself as the source of feedback, reporting
on the visible effects of the trainee's acts, letting him know if
they worked out or not. In this way the trainee can make a conscious effort to associate his feels with the outcomes reported by
the instructor. And he can concentrate his awareness on the
feels without the intrusion of evidence from whatever other
sense—in this case, vision—had served him but is now blocked
off.

To move the trainee into the final stage of relying on his
kinesthetic feedback alone, the instructor can serve simply as a
confirmer of the trainee's own kinesthetic signals. That is, he
can quiz the trainee as to the "feel" of the act: Did it feel right or
not? And then he can let the trainee know if the effect was actually good or poor as it showed up visibly at the contact point.
A consistent reply identifying the right feel with a successful
outcome will indicate the trainee's readiness to use the kinesthetic channel in the unassisted performance of the job. Confidence in the kinesthetic feedback appears to be a necessary
precondition for abandonment of visual feedback. The instructor, however, should be careful not to force a reliance on feel
when continued reliance on vision is more efficient or when feel
is not the appropriate or safe means of picking up signals.

In the case of subroutines of the task which must be performed simultaneously, the training problem often boils down
to the matter of using separate sensory channels for the subroutines. Otherwise the demand on visual attention particularly is
beyond the trainee's capacity; he cannot focus on two things at
once. A suggested procedure is to concentrate in our training

on one of the subroutines until the trainee can proceed through it "automatically" by reference to kinesthetic feedback. At this point, we can attempt to join the second subroutine to the first; we can free the trainee to use visual feedback for the second.

For example, if a sewing machine operator has to reach and pre-position a second piece while she completes the sewing on the first, she cannot rely on vision for both operations. Consequently, one must be taught until some degree of reliance on feel is achieved before the other is imposed on it. In such cases a troublesome decision needs to be made as to the most efficient channel of feedback for each of the separate subroutines. In our example, this question must be resolved: Should the trainee be trained to sew by feel or to pre-position the cloth by feel?

The Bridging Process

In the connecting of responses or sets of responses, two processes apparently come into play:

1. The development of an economy in the perceptual evidence used for determining that the "now" responses are working out
2. An expediting, through anticipation, of the sizing-up of what lies ahead.

In regard to the first process, the skilled operator appears not to wait until the full available set of signals runs its course. A key perception or an early perception seems to serve to move him confidently through the responses by assuring him that the outcome will be good and to free him up for a view of what lies ahead and the establishment of a "set" for handling it. Perhaps a reliance on feel as the last part of the feedback is what actually occurs. In any event, the employee does not seem to wait until all the available feedback is played out before he approaches or begins or prepares for his next series of moves.

Let us look at a few examples from jobs. A battery filler (who puts full bobbins of yarn in a container, called a battery, attached to the loom) positions each bobbin by fitting the butt end into a round slot and inserting the tip end into a spring clip. After such positioning of the bobbin, her next step is to position a length of yarn (previously unwound from the bobbin) over a round projection of the battery. When a battery filler reaches a high level of skill, she pays little observable attention to the position of the bobbin tip in relation to the spring clip as she inserts it. If the butt end is seated in the slot—this she checks—she can apparently rely on the tip end to fall into place in the spring clip without the need to check it. So instead of attending to the spring clip, she proceeds to position the yarn while the tip of the bobbin goes into the clip.

Similarly, an assembler who inserts a part into a subassembly by sliding it into a slotted recess will focus her visual attention on the entering position of the part, but after it starts to move into place she will prepare to start or will actually start her next move without waiting for the full part to come to rest in final position.

Again, a weaver who is drawing (threading) warp yarn ends through eyelets or dents with a reed hook will start the end through the opening and assure himself that it is in the right place but will then complete the move to pull it through without paying any obvious attention to it. Meanwhile, being assured on the first check that it will come through all right, he proceeds with the left hand to position the next yarn end for drawing through as he completes pulling the first end through with the reed hook in his right hand.

These examples may represent a close juxtaposition of motions rather than genuinely simultaneous motions. With such a quick bridging-over as to give the appearance of simultaneity, the gain in speed is obvious.

An instructor need not await the trainee's pleasure in zeroing-in on the key items of feedback. He can help the trainee to identify them, can illustrate that they will serve sufficiently to assure a satisfactory completion of the particular set of responses, and can identify the advance signals to which the trainee should refer in preparation for the next set of responses. And, most importantly, he can give the trainee guided practice in the use of the foreshortened "result cues" and the "anticipatory cues." If kinesthetic feedback is involved in the learning process at this point, some such approach as previously suggested may help.

A word of caution is in order. Often a trainee, in anticipation of what he must do next, will be less alert to the current feedback or fail to use it; and thus his present act will suffer. He may stumble before he reaches the bridge if he looks across it too soon. Here again the instructor can assist, perhaps through the use of timing-cues which will keep the trainee from moving prematurely.

Anticipating Signals in a Monitoring Task

If the job involves a monitoring or patrolling function with required action when certain conditions are observed, teaching the trainee to anticipate signals may help him to improve his skill and speed of performance. When the signs telling the trainee to do certain things are scattered in time and place (that is, occur at random times or appear any place in a wide area), it is difficult to alert the trainee so that he can pick them up quickly and proceed to take the indicated actions without undue delay. If the trainee, because of the nature of the job, cannot predict when and where things will occur, the instructor can be specific as to what the signals are (what to look for) but, in regard to anticipation, can do little more than produce in the trainee a stage of "general alert."

If signals tend to come together or to be somewhat regularly spaced (in terms of time intervals or location), the instructor can help the trainee gain speed by helping him to anticipate. For example, if a certain mechanical trouble is revealed by two related symptoms, the repairman trainee should be alerted to expect one when the other occurs. Again, if most types of common defects occur at certain places in the manufactured item or material, the inspector trainee should be taught to expect them there and to give those sections of the item adequate attention. Or if a defect tends to repeat itself from one piece to another at a fixed location, the trainee should be made aware of the "repeats" and the probability that the defect will turn up again at a predictable location so that he will be on the "watch" for it. In such cases the "alert" can be very specific in terms not only of what will show up, but also when and where to look for it.

The things that occur on certain jobs are somewhat unpredictable. But often an adequate analysis of the job will reveal a substantial degree of order or regularity in the signals telling the trainee that an action must be taken. If such order does exist and can be uncovered and made known to the trainee, he is in a better position to anticipate the signs and to initiate his response quickly.

Timing or Pacing the Trainee

The timing or pacing of the trainee can be a technique of pressure disruptive to performance, or it can be a constructive source of feedback motivating to the trainee. The effect depends largely on when these techniques are introduced and how they are used. The more crucial decision probably concerns "when."

If the timing or pacing attempts are made too early, at a stage when the trainee's performance is weak in the use of perceptual feedback, the trainee may be pushing for greater speed in somewhat rigid elements—moves and reaches—which may not respond significantly to heightened effort. There simply is not enough in the performance for the stopwatch to work on. In such a case the trainee may feel heavy pressure to seek shortcuts by desperate trial-and-error methods. His general performance will tend to suffer. He may do less well at what he is already presumed to know; and if he picks up anything new, it is likely to be a poor habit which will later require correction.

The earliest stage at which timing or pacing appears to be appropriate is when the trainee has mastered not only the basic motion pattern but the use of at least the intermediate types of perceptual feedback. We should reserve our timing or pacing for a somewhat rounded performance which includes enough of the skill ingredients for potentially high-level work. But still we must be alert to any disruptive effects which a direct measure of speed might bring about.

Concerning the use of these techniques:

1. *Timing* should be related to goals within the reach of the trainee. Timing periods should be long enough and repeated so that the trainee can see signs of improvement. The author's personal experience with assembly tasks seems to indicate that enough cycles should be timed in one period to effect some improvement in speed (even a small movement will do), but we should permit the trainee a considerable period to proceed on his own between timing periods. Timing on alternate days has proved to be a reasonable schedule.

Information on time taken should be given to the trainee immediately upon the completion of each cycle of the task or subtask being timed. That is, a consistent feedback schedule appears to be the most effective during the timing periods.

Breaking the job into tasks and timing separate tasks not only may help in the general improvement in speed but also has the advantage of determining where the slowness is concentrated. For such diagnostic purposes, the division of tasks into subtasks for separate timing is even more useful, provided the subtasks are not too small. A recommended procedure is not to time the trainee on repeated performances of small elements of the task but to secure separate timings on the subparts as the trainee repeats the larger task.

If slowness is detected it does not necessarily indicate the need for greater effort. It may instead require us to provide the trainee with help in whatever genuine aspects of skill—often perceptual aspects—the trainee lacks or is weak in.

2. *Pacing* is a natural and easy technique to use in jobs involving partners (jointly processing a common product, for example). The pacer must be careful not to step up his pace too quickly or to fail to step it up when the trainee is ready. The trainee's readiness is the main criterion to go by. Some "settling" is required at a certain pace, but we should be wary about prolonging the settling and thus fixing the performance at that pace.

An ordered progression seems to be needed to make pacing work. An arrangement which pairs a trainee for a considerable time with an instructor (who will move him forward gradually) appears to bring better results than an alternating schedule which shuttles the trainee between an experienced partner and another trainee. The latter schedule permits the trainee to revert to a slower pace even when he is capable of sustaining a faster.

In jobs not involving partners, pacing arrangements are more difficult to devise. However, an instructor, with a little ingenuity, can often rig up a signal to tell the trainee how far along he should be in the task at certain intervals of time and when he should be completing the task. The instructor should be careful not to give a signal which will distract the trainee from his task. For example, he should not require the trainee to look up (to see where the pacer has progressed in the task) if the trainee must concentrate his visual attention on elements of the task itself. In such instances an auditory signal is in order.

Organizing the Job

In jobs which involve several machines and a variety of job tasks, the development of skill requires that the trainee know not only how to perform the separate tasks but when to perform them in order to stay "on top of the job." Numerous demands are made on his time; he must learn to parcel out his time in such a way as to fulfill all the demands of the job.

Of course, the first step in training a new employee in this type of job is to teach him how to perform each task. It is pointless (or at least, premature) for him to learn when the tasks need to be performed if he does not know how to perform them. On those jobs which do not permit the separation of job tasks from the regular routine for special practice, the trainee learns some degree of job organization while he is learning the job tasks. But even in these cases the heavier emphasis at the first should be on the learning of the tasks.

Types of Job Tasks

Machine-tending jobs are usually made up of a number of different types or aspects of tasks such as the following:

1. *Demanding tasks,* which must be performed as they come up in order to avoid loss of production. When a machine needs

material fed to it or finished material or pieces taken from it, the operator cannot delay his performance of the tasks if he is to prevent downtime or loss of efficiency. Material must get to the machine and be removed from it.

2. *Job procedures* for the "demanding" tasks. Part of the schedule of the operator's tasks is imposed by the machine itself. It is ready to be unloaded after a certain running period; the processing is finished at this point. The supply of material positioned at the machine lasts for a certain time, then must be replenished. In addition, the operator must handle a certain number of units in loading and unloading the machine in order to assure that he carries out the "cycle" tasks efficiently. And in many instances he has to have his materials lined up in a certain amount or number and in a convenient storage space in order to move quickly to the task.

3. *Preventive tasks.* These involve patrolling the machines with the intent of spotting conditions that will result in later difficulties if uncorrected. The frequency and thoroughness of such patrolling are essential to maintaining quality and efficiency.

4. *Corrective tasks.* Patrolling is also done to detect conditions "after the fact"—damages or losses already incurred—so that early correction will reduce the loss of output or prevent further damage. Of course, once the conditions have been discovered, corrective actions must be taken.

5. *Housekeeping and maintenance tasks.* Many jobs include cleaning chores which are required in order to avoid mechanical and quality problems. The machinery must be kept free of an accumulation of waste, dirt, grease, etc. If cleaning is to serve its purpose, it must be done not only thoroughly but also often enough. The schedule of cleaning is therefore important. Some types of cleaning must be done once per shift, others once per day (dividing the machinery among shifts), others once per week, etc.

Some operating jobs require the replacement of minor machine parts. Again, the scheduling of such activities is important.

If an operator must signal the repairman when certain machine symptoms or malfunctions develop, he must know what the symptoms are and how the information is to be passed along to the repairman (posting of a notice, word of mouth, or whatever). When "service tasks" (aside from the mechanical) are the responsibility of other employees, the operator must know when and how to get the word to these people that their services are needed so as to minimize machine downtime.

Teaching the Organization of the Job

The "doing" of virtually all of the types of tasks listed above can be taught by practice in the tasks and by the use of the techniques discussed earlier. Teaching job organization, however, requires the teaching of:

1. The schedules for the performance of the various separate tasks. (We will assume, for our purpose, that the use of performance aids is impractical or inefficient and that the schedules must be learned.)
2. A set of priorities which will tell the trainee what to do when the schedules conflict, when two or more job tasks are required to be performed at the same time. The demanding and corrective tasks, for example, usually take priority over the preventive and housekeeping tasks.

The schedules and priorities need to be known "in the head" as well as "in the hands"—and, preferably, if a logical order of training is to be followed, they will be learned first in the head. That is, we will first teach the trainee what those schedules and priorities are and then teach the trainee to follow the schedules and priorities on the job itself.

Training Arrangements

A recommended training arrangement for dealing with job organization would proceed in the following manner:

1. Have the trainee memorize the schedules (machine cycle times, cleaning schedules, patrolling schedules, etc.). We will have previously taught the trainee how to do the cleaning, what to look for in patrolling, and what to do about the difficulties spotted. That is, the "how" aspect of the tasks will have been mastered; we are concerned now only with the "when."

Teach the trainee these schedules by repetition and testing. Have him "overlearn" the schedules. Stop the training only when he has recited (or written) the schedules correctly a number of times.

2. Have the trainee memorize the order of priorities, again by repetition and testing.

3. Present the trainee with priority problems. Ask him what he would do in situations involving conflicting demands. Draw up a whole series of such situations, covering all common contingencies, and quiz him concerning the correct order of handling. Again, stay with this approach until overlearning occurs.

4. After the schedules and the order of priorities have become well fixed in the trainee's mind, take him to the job to practice applying them, so that the learning can advance to the crucial stage of performance.

Have the trainee, under the instructor's guidance, perform the job tasks in the regular routine, that is, facing the problems of schedules and priorities on the job itself. Have the trainee explain why he has decided to perform the particular task as he goes from task to task. Be sure to correct wrong decisions or choices on the part of the trainee. Continue such quizzing until the trainee has faced (and explained his choice of action concerning) most of the situations he is likely to encounter. At this point, drop the quizzing but observe the trainee for an additional period of sufficient length to assure that he can continue to keep the job properly organized.

As a useful variation of this approach, the instructor can introduce the trainee to the job at a more leisurely pace (after step 3). He can have the trainee observe him in the regular routine of the job for a short period and then have the trainee direct the instructor's work, requiring the trainee to give related explanations of why he would have the instructor perform each task at the time he decides. After this introduction, the trainee could begin performing the job in the regular routine under the instructor's guidance (picking up at step 4 above).

If the trainee has difficulty performing certain tasks or develops job-organization problems (failure to stay up with the demands of the job even with adequate skill in each task), special instructions should be given directed at the cause of the trouble as diagnosed by the instructor or supervisor.

Required Size of Assignment

It is obvious that job organization skills—the actual using of schedules and priorities—cannot be taught effectively unless the trainee is given a slice of the job large enough to require organization. A machine-operator trainee assigned to too small a part of the job will have too little to do to require any planning or decision making in the use of his time. He will rarely encounter a situation of conflicting tasks and therefore will get little practice in assigning priorities. The patrolling tasks, so important in the running of a full multi-machine job, become simply a gesture, and a somewhat meaningless one, if there is almost nothing to patrol. In short, the development of job-organization skill requires practice, and such practice can best be provided in situations actually requiring the use of job-organization skill—that is, in a substantial machine assignment.

Once the trainee has acquired ample skill in the performance of the separate tasks of the job, the recommended approach is to move him into a significant part of a full assignment of machines, under instruction, with the purpose of teaching him to organize the job. The idea is to have the trainee assume all of the required duties in this workload through the acquisition of organizational skills as applied in the regular routine of the job. Then he proceeds to a substantially larger workload, and the integrating process resumes until he encompasses the new load. Thus he advances in relatively large steps to the full job by bringing the added segments, along with the prior portions, under his effective control rather than making a laborious climb from a small beginning assignment through insignificant periodic increases to the final full workload. Of course, the readiness of the individual trainee, as evidenced by his achievement of performance criteria such as efficiency, and the degree of complexity in the job are compelling influences on the decisions concerning progression. But to require a multiplicity of way stations when a few will serve is to prolong the climb unnecessarily and to discourage it. The full load then becomes a remote and unattainable goal in many such cases. (A similar adverse effect may arise from unjustified delays in advancing a trainee to the next level.) The more efficient procedure in teaching the trainee to pull everything together after he has acquired good skill in the job tasks is to start with a sizable workload and, through efficient development of the trainee's organizational skill and careful assessments of his readiness for successive stages, to advance him by reasonably large increments to an early mastery of the full assignment.

In Summary: Bringing the Parts Together

In order for an instructor to teach job organization he must take the same care and the same systematic approach as he used in teaching the separate job tasks. He must define what is to be taught; the various aspects of organizing a multi-machine job which we listed earlier must be specifically written for the particular job (its patrolling schedule, cleaning schedule, priorities, procedures, etc.). Arrangements and techniques for teaching job organization such as those suggested here must be made for the specific job. The idea that job-organization skills can come "only with experience" is not good enough for us. We should arrange and direct the trainee's experience, through conscious training efforts, so as to teach him quickly how to "stay on top of the job."

Coping With Abnormal Conditions

Unfortunately, job conditions are subject to changes, often changes which are hard to predict. The plan of action (the organizational arrangements) which serves to keep the job under the employee's control in normal circumstances will not enable him to cope with the adverse and emergency situations that arise. That is, the usual set of priorities and normal allocations of time involving the various job tasks will no longer do. In effect, a new game plan is called for.

Our training arrangements should prepare the employee, insofar as practical, to cope with new conditions. At the very beginning stage of defining the job for training purposes we should analyze the possible contingencies which are likely to arise. A form such as the one shown below is helpful in identi-

CHECKLIST FOR ANALYZING "COPING" REQUIREMENTS OF JOB

JOB —————— DEPARTMENT —————— MILL ——————

	Situations That May Arise	Likelihood	Problems Caused	What You Should Do
1. Incoming material—amount				
2. Incoming material—condition				
3. Supplies and equipment—amount (boxes, wagons, trucks, cans, quills, etc.)				
4. Supplies and equipment—condition				
5. Machinery—mechanical running condition (effect on efficiency)				
6. Machinery—effect on materials				
7. Changes in surrounding conditions (humidity, heat, etc.)				
8. Services provided by other employees (service operators, fixers, battery fillers, etc.)				
9. How job is left by preceding shift				
10. Special or emergency job assignments (samples, special orders, etc.)				

fying those abnormal difficulties which may occur with materials, equipment, machinery, and supportive services on the employee's own shift and with adverse situations which may carry over from the previous shift to make the job less manageable. Beyond identifying possible problems, the analysis should indicate the "coping" actions required of the employee in facing each kind of problem.

The actions of the employee are likely to involve one or more of the following:

1. Making a distinction between the conditions which the employee can correct (or make tolerable) and conditions which should be called to the attention of someone else.

2. Informing the right person and informing him in terms which will be helpful in attempting to improve the situation. The right person might be a repairman, a service operator, or a supervisor.

3. Directly attacking the problem by such steps as:

   (1) Adjusting the schedule of job activities—basically a matter of deciding which tasks or activities can be omitted, minimized, or delayed so as to keep the major operation moving as well as possible and to permit a concentration of effort and time on the troublesome condition.

   (2) Taking whatever action is required to clear up the condition or to make compensatory moves to minimize its effects.

Of course, it is not enough to identify the contingencies and define the coping mechanisms for the trainee. This is a minimum gesture, though important in itself since it permits the trainee to anticipate problems and to avoid the shock and discouragement which their unexpected emergence may bring. The practice in coping is important, and we should arrange to coach the trainee in performance itself. If certain of the conditions occur during the training period, we have a ready-made opportunity for training. If conditions do not occur—and by their very nature they may not—within the training period, it may be possible to contrive their occurrence or by simulation run the trainee through the indicated steps. In addition, help should be available on the job itself, on an on-call basis at least, for a sufficient time to insure that the emergencies encountered by the trainee are dealt with.

Finally, we should equip the trainee with the anticipatory skills (largely perceptual) and the knowledge which will prevent certain problems from developing or will nip a problem in the bud. A patrolling or inspecting routine and a clear idea of what to look for may serve to keep trouble at a minimum. The unpredictable, we often find, is largely predictable if we can detect the signs.

CASES FOR DISCUSSION

The following cases are intended to illustrate the general point that learning continues over a long period of time before ultimate job skill is achieved and that training efforts should be made along the way to expedite this development. More specifically, the cases hopefully will indicate that the particular means used to assist the learning process should be diagnostically aimed at the valid needs of the trainee at his stage of learning, that an exclusive reliance on timing the employee and stimulating greater effort is an inadequate and often misdirected gesture. The discussion can concentrate on how we might better address ourselves to the problem of helping the trainee develop speed and organize his job—the things he must do if he is to run the job with genuine skill.

Case 1

A new supervisor explained a training dilemma in the following way: "I give up. If I do A, it turns out that B would have been better. If I do B, then A is better.

"The hardest part of the machine-operating job in my department is to reach and pre-position a second piece of stock for processing while you're finishing off the first. The reach is an 'internal element,' as they call it, and has got to be performed while the processing is going on. But it sure as the devil can't be taught that way. A trainee would need four eyes, each separately focused, to do it all at the same time.

"I know enough to realize that the learner has to sort of get the processing under control to some extent before working on the reach. But to what extent? That's my problem.

"The first woman I taught I kept on the processing for a day and then tried to get her to make the reach while she was doing the processing. God, it tore her all up. Not only couldn't she make the reach but she couldn't do the processing right, either.

"I learned my lesson—or I thought I did. The next woman who came in I kept on the processing for a full week. For a whole week I just had her forget the reach. Then when I was sure she was ready I tried to train her to make the reach at the same time she was doing the processing. By heavens, she couldn't do it. I couldn't force her to do it. I'm stuck with her. She finishes a piece, then reaches for the next. That's it. Forever and ever, I guess.

"I'm afraid to think of the next one. What should I do with her?"

Question: What advice would you give the supervisor concerning the training of the next woman? How can she be helped to incorporate all the parts of the task? What can the supervisor do now about the second woman he has already "trained"?

Case 2

In Department B the operations are performed by pairs of employees working together; each member of a pair will work on the same item but at opposite ends of it. As one aspect of the training plan, the supervisor at certain intervals would team a new worker with a skilled partner as a pacing device. This arrangement appeared to bring results, so much so that the supervisor decided he could make better use of a good thing. He decided that, after the beginning stage of teaching the motion pattern, he would use the pacing arrangement more or less continuously. The average time required to bring a learner to piece-rate production on the job was 10 weeks. He determined to cut this training time in half with his concentrated pacing approach.

With his next trainee he succeeded beyond his most optimistic expectations. The new trainee made the piece rate after three weeks. The supervisor was so pleased he called her in to congratulate her. She replied, "I'm glad someone is happy about this; I'm certainly not. In fact, I'm quitting. No one ought to have to work that hard to make a living."

Question: What went wrong with this "good thing"? What suggestion would you make to the supervisor concerning his training in the future, particularly his pacing arrangements?

Case 3

A supervisor explained how he tried to use a "law of learning."

"I don't know why, when you use one of these so-called laws of learning, it doesn't work. Like the idea of spacing the training.

"When this new operator first came on the job I kept her at it pretty steadily for a week or so, and her progress was pretty good. She was coming up a little each day.

"But I could tell she was getting too heavy a dose of it; you can't push people too hard. So I decided to use her around on other operations—killing two birds with one stone, you might say. She was helping me fill in when other people were out and at the same time she was getting some relief from her own job. I shifted her back and forth. On an average, she spent about half her time on her own job and half on the relief jobs. That's the way it went for a week. But do you know what happened to her learning curve? It flattened out like a pancake!

"And they call these things laws of learning!"

Question: What do you think about this supervisor's application of "laws of learning"? What would you recommend that he do now?

Case 4

Here is a complaint from another supervisor:

"I like an engineering approach to training. A real system. One thing at a time so you know where you stand. You bring a trainee up to standard; you time him until he makes it, on each element of the job. One at a time. Then you know he can do it; then you know he's ready to take on the full job. You just move him into the full job when he has proved he can perform each element at standard time.

"But lately I don't know. You just can't rely on some people. There are exceptions to every rule. I brought a new man along this way just last week, and on Monday I told him he was ready and assigned him to the job. Know what he said? The darned fool said, 'Ready for what?' This is Thursday and he still hasn't run the job. And I know he can do it. I have the recorded timings I made on him last week on each of the job elements to prove it. He hit standard or better on all of them."

Question: What do you think of the foreman's approach to the training of the new man? Why wasn't the employee ready? What would you suggest to the foreman now?

Case 5

A supervisor described his method of drawing a learning curve and his experience in using it:

"There's nothing mysterious about a learning curve. I just used common sense in drawing one up for my main piece-rate job. I took an average output figure for trainees after the first week—when we could put a finger on individual output—and then drew a straight diagonal line to the piece-rate level of output, which I pegged at the eight-week mark. On this job the piece-rate level is 45 units per hour, and the average output after one week is 10 units per hour. I drew a line which cut through 15 units after two weeks, 20 units after three weeks, 25 after four, etc., on up in equal steps, week by week, to the final point of 45 units after eight weeks.

"The reason I use eight weeks on this particular curve is because that's when I want the new trainee to reach the piece-rate level. That's not the average time taken to make the rate on this job; usually it takes about 10 weeks. But I cut the time a little short, just to give the new trainees a little added incentive, you know.

"I've noticed in using the curve, though, that a new trainee will stay above it the first few weeks and then fall below it. It's not supposed to work out that way, and it's a hard thing on the trainees when you review it with them. At first they're encouraged, then they're discouraged. I figure there must be some weaknesses in our training program. I've asked one of our training men to come over and discuss how we can strengthen our program in the second month to bring the trainees up to where they ought to be."

Question: If you were the training man, what would you suggest to this supervisor? What questions would you raise about a curve that does not curve?

Case 6

A supervisor called in an industrial engineer to review the job methods being used by two trainees assigned to a complex assembly job which required a long series of motions and numerous exact positionings of parts. The trainees were in the middle of their fourth week on the job; the normal learning time to reach piece-rate production was four weeks. The production of the trainees was about two-thirds of the piece-work quota.

The engineer's report to the supervisor read, in part: "These trainees are using the correct motion pattern but are just slow about it. The problem is one of enforcing adequate effort. They should not be permitted to operate at their present level of output."

Question: If you were in this supervisor's position, what would you do at this point? Is effort the only answer? How can you bring speed into the performance of a precise operation like this one?

Case 7

A supervisor explained how he used stopwatch timings to move his trainees along. "You see, the main thing about timing an operation, the main purpose is so that I know how the trainee is doing. Of course, I don't keep it all to myself. I think it's a good idea to let the trainee know how long it takes him to complete a task. And I do tell him, but in a general way. After I finish timing him on a number of cycles, I tell him how he did on an average—I cite an average figure—and how close that average is to the goal, whatever the goal happens to be for his length of training. The goal could be the expected level on the learning curve if he's pretty new or the piece-rate level if he has been around for awhile.

"But this business of telling him his time after each and every cycle, that's just too much. It's not really needed to push him along and it makes him nervous. Besides, it's not really his business. It's mine most of all. I'm responsible for moving him along, and I'm the one who has to know where he stands. That's what the training is all about."

Question: Whose business is it? How should information on stopwatch times be used?

Case 8

Another supervisor commented on the timing of trainees, referring in particular to a "disorganized fellow" whose performance after timing left a great deal to be desired. Here's how the supervisor explained it: "I try to start a new man out right. That means staying with him until he really knows the motion pattern of the job. Then the experience will carry him along in regard to skill. And timing him with the stop watch will bring his speed along. And there you have it, both sides covered, skill and speed.

"That's what I've been doing with this last fellow, but I've just about given up on him. I never saw such a disorganized fellow; maybe he just doesn't have the coordination needed on this job. I've timed him on three different occasions, getting readings on a lot of cycles each time. And each time the same thing happened. He went flying harum-scarum through the method, if you call it a method after he fractured it, not paying a darn bit of attention to anything as he went, and turning out some of the worst work I've ever seen. A batch of scrap, that's what he turned out, not a first-quality piece in the whole lot. I don't understand it. I know he knows the method. And he's not the nervous type."

Question: What advice would you give this supervisor in regard to the timing of this operator? Why, in your opinion, was the operator having problems when he was timed? What training help does he need, if any?

Chapter 10

Measuring Performance

Two of the principal reasons for measuring the performance of the trainee are:

1. To have evidence of progress to pass on to the trainee.
   As discussed earlier, it is important to learning (and to
   motivation for learning) that the trainee know where he
   stands.

2. To have a basis for diagnosing the trainee's difficulties
   so that he will have a better opportunity to improve in
   the event his progress is unsatisfactory or his skill is developing unevenly from task to task, so that both he and
   the instructor will know what aspects of the job to concentrate on.

These purposes go hand in hand. It is not enough to tell
the trainee that his performance is weak without providing him
with the help needed to improve. What specific aspects is he
weak in? What can be done about it? These questions need to
be discussed in the process of giving progress information to
the trainee, and arrangements must be made to give the trainee
the help he requires.

Thus, discussions go hand in hand with measurements of
progress. Unless the trainee is made aware of how he measures
up, the measurements are of limited use in helping him to
learn.

The instructor should be discussing the trainee's performance in very specific terms and very frequently as one of the on-
going instructional techniques. (See discussion of feedback.) In
addition, the instructor should summarize the trainee's progress at daily intervals and discuss each measure of progress with
the trainee. At a later time, after the trainee has been put on his
own, a supervisor should continue the measurements and dis-

cussions, though at greater intervals of time, until the trainee reaches the piece-rate level of performance (or day-rate, whichever applies). Even in the earlier stages of training it is advisable for the supervisor to participate, along with the instructor, in the measuring of the trainee's progress and the discussions with him concerning progress.

Types of Measurements and When to Make Them

Measurements of progress can take various shapes and will differ from one stage of learning to another.

1. In the early stage of training the main purpose of the instructor is to teach the method of each task to the trainee. Consequently, the instructor will be looking for evidence of progress in following the method. He can gather this evidence by observing the trainee and by making a count of the number of times consecutively that the trainee works through the particular task without error.

The measurement should be aimed at some standard or criterion of performance (a so-called target) which represents "overlearning"; hence we would concentrate on method until the trainee can perform the task many times without error.

2. At a later stage we are normally concerned with development of speed (realizing that there is an overlap between stages and that the job method itself will include aspects of speed). Our measurement, therefore, is of speed; and our goal is the completion of the trained task repeatedly within a target time.

In the early part of this stage of training, the goal should be modest; but before the concentration on speed is eased up, the trainee should be brought to (or near to) the required piece-rate or day-rate speed for the particular task. Otherwise the later concentration on job organization will not pay off; the trainee will still be laboring with inefficient execution of the tasks when he should be occupied with schedules and priorities. When the time arrives to do a task, he will be held up too long in the task itself.

If it is impractical or imprudent to time the trainee (as it often is when the training is given in the production department), a fairly accurate judgment of speed can be obtained by observation and by relating the trainee's performance to the pacing arrangement or device.

3. At the stage when the trainee is learning job organization, the view of his performance should focus primarily on his development of skill in staying abreast of the job. It should deal with specifics, such as: What is the trainee doing at the right time? At the wrong time? What particular aspects of the job are holding him up (if job demands pile up)? Method and speed in performance of separate job tasks need to be observed to some extent during this period to assure that the trainee is not slowed up by a loss of skill (change in method, loss of speed) in the performance of the tasks themselves.

Since this stage is a preparation for placing the trainee on his own, a target in terms of keeping the full job running satisfactorily needs to be established. Efficiency and quality measurements are sometimes available, and targets can be set on these indices. In addition, the trainee could be required to run the full job himself for progressively longer periods of time (with progressive goals) until he can manage it continuously without help from the instructor.

If the trainee is placed on a partial workload (preferably a substantial load) and works up to a full load in this stage, it is possible to set up targets at each point in his progression, the attainment of which will satisfy requirements for taking on more machines. The targets could be efficiency or quality goals and the goal of keeping up with the assigned workload for a certain period of time. The measurements of progress would be in the same terms: efficiency percentages, quality figures, and the length of time he can sustain the assigned workload.

The targets and the measurements of performance that go along with them should provide a logical training progression from the beginning of the training period to the point when the trainee goes on his own. That is, the trainee should be considered "qualified" to move from one stage to another in terms of his successfully meeting the performance targets. Since trainees progress at different rates, the time required to work through the various stages or tasks will be different from trainee to trainee. Although the particular training plan may include instructional schedules (designated periods of time to be devoted to certain progressive stages of learning or particular tasks), these schedules should be varied by the instructor for individual trainees in the light of the individual's progress. The object is not to keep the trainee at a task or stage for a fixed period but to keep him there until he is qualified (meets target) to move ahead.

4. When a trainee finally is qualified to go on his own, his progress should be followed by a continuation of measurements. Since he then usually is assigned to a full job and has the sole responsibility for it, it is easier to measure his performance than at earlier stages. If he is on a piece-rate job, efficiency or output figures are usually available. Often quality data (number or percentage of defective pieces) are also available. Beyond these measurements, however, the supervisor should observe the trainee often enough to assure that difficulties of method, speed, or job organization are spotted. A periodic rating of the trainee on these factors should be made to supplement the output and quality data. And the supervisor should discuss the information on progress at periodic intervals with the trainee until the trainee consistently performs the full job at the required piece-rate or day-rate level and meets quality and other standards.

Requirements for a Good Measurement

If we are truly to measure a trainee's performance, particularly at the late stages of learning when efficiency and quality indices are often available, we must be assured that our gauge is capable of giving a valid picture. The measurements must meet certain criteria. Specifically, they should be:

1. *Pertinent to the job or to job requirements.* If, for example, quality is of little importance in a job, we should not measure the trainee's progress by means of a quality index. Output or efficiency is usually pertinent, unless the trainee has little or no control over it.

2. *Something we can attribute to the trainee.* That is, what shows up in the measurement should represent something the trainee does significantly control. A sewing machine operator

has control over output; we accept output, then, as a measure of performance. On the other hand, the amount of production from a machine-paced job is often outside the control of the machine tender or operator. The degree of control is also reduced in many machine operating jobs to the extent that output is influenced by the work of maintenance men and auxiliary or "service" help. In such instances, output figures are a questionable measure of the job performance of machine operators.

Care should be taken to separate what the trainee does from what the instructor does in judging trainee performance if both are working jointly on a machine or set of machines. The trainee should not be judged by the instructor's efficiency or output in such cases.

3. *A typical representation of how the trainee is doing.* Ratings by means of observation often fail as a means of measurement because the observations do not cover enough of the trainee's work. They are often not long enough; they are likely to pick up an unusual or extraordinary incident and exaggerate it. If observational ratings are used, the observations should extend over a period long enough to give a picture which is representative of the way the trainee really performs the tasks of the job.

There is, of course, the danger of making a rating which does not truly reflect performance, no matter how long the observation. Instructors and supervisors who serve as raters should be wary of such errors of rating as leniency, or placing almost everyone at or near average, or rating the trainee high in other aspects of the job because he is outstanding in one aspect.

4. *Free from bias.* The measurement should be based on job performance rather than on aspects of the trainee's conduct, appearance, or temperament having little or no effect on job performance. Each of us has prejudices which are likely to show up in subjective measurements such as ratings.

Even in objective measurements (actual figures on output, quality, etc.) we tend to get a lopsided picture if we play up the unimportant aspects of the job and give too little weight to the important aspects.

In summary, if the measurements of job performance are

to serve as a real learning tool (used for motivation and diagnosis), they should be true and reliable measures. Otherwise
the training efforts which evolve from them will be misdirected.

Diagnosing Learning Problems

The measures we have been discussing—indications of adherence to method and of speed of execution early in the learning period and indications of output and quality later—will
serve to reveal the presence of difficulties in the development
of job competence. But it will take a fine-grained analysis to pin-
point more precisely the aspect of learning troubling the trainee and to identify the causes of his difficulty. In short, we need
to move from measurement to diagnosis before taking corrective action.

If our observations and measures show that the trainee is
making errors in the motion pattern or is slow in performing a
task, it is premature to drill him strictly in motions in the first
case or to elicit greater effort from him through pacing in the
second. A truly analytic view would require a close look at the
perceptual aspect of his performance, since we can be reasonably sure that refinements in motion pattern and gains in speed
are dependent upon efficient use of feedback. So it would pay
us to examine the trainee's feedback "system."

We can raise these questions regarding each feedback
point used by the trainee:

- Where is the trainee's attention focused?
- What sensory channel is used? Vision, hearing, or what?
- What information is obtained?

And, pointing toward corrective action, we can ask additional
questions aimed at identifying the means of increasing the efficiency of the trainee's feedback:

- Can his perception time be shortened? Information
  picked up and processed faster? Is this checkpoint necessary?
- Are there better alternatives (using the same sensory
  channel)?
- Should a shift be made to a different channel? If so, is the
  trainee ready?

Close scrutiny of performance may reveal that the trainee is performing consecutively certain motions or subtasks which should be performed simultaneously. In such instance, the diagnostic questions to be raised would again deal with perceptual feedback since we know that the reliance on the same sensory channel for feedback involving subtasks will require a delay in execution between them. So the pertinent questions are:

- What sensory channels is the trainee using for feedback of the motions which should be made simultaneously? (Is he using vision for both, for example?)
- What sensory channels should be used for each in order to permit simultaneous performance? (Can he shift to the kinesthetic sense for one?)

It may be found that transitional moves linking up tasks or subtasks are ragged or slow. Again, the key to the trouble may be feedback. We would raise the questions:

- Is the trainee holding too long to the feedback signalling completion of the first subtask?
- Is the trainee looking forward to the next task (anticipating signals for it) soon enough?

Later in the learning period the intent of our diagnosis would tend to shift from the detection of errant performance involving motions and speed and their perceptual components (though we would continue our attention to these aspects) to the identification of obstacles to the trainee's organization of the full job. We would examine the evidence of his success or failure in fitting together all of the job tasks, each of which he can perform adequately, into a total context representing job competence and reflected in efficiency and quality of output. If these later indices genuinely point to the presence of a problem, assuming the trainee has not retrogressed in task method or speed, we need to raise such questions as these:

- How does the trainee distribute his time among the various job tasks?
- Does he use a system of priorities to handle conflicting demands (two or more job tasks requiring his attention at the same time)?

Sometimes major objectives of the job themselves, for example, output and quality, are seen by the trainee as conflicting requirements. His development of the speed necessary for satisfactory output may be hindered or his full use of acquired speed may be inhibited by a concern for quality. Our search for causes should take this possibility into account.

If the trainee has a job in which operating conditions may change—the running properties of the material, for example—we should raise the pertinent questions:

- How does the trainee cope with changed conditions?
- Do the changing conditions have the effect of so disorganizing the job that it gets beyond him?

Finally, there is motivation, which may affect learning in any of its stages. As a practical matter, the trainer may find it necessary to regard a trainee's poor progress early in the learning period as a learning problem. It is often difficult at the early stages to sift the evidence so as to separate the effects on progress of motivational influences from the effects of other influences. The competent trainer uses sound instructional techniques and trusts that their motivational properties, particularly the reinforcement imbedded in feedback, will serve to keep the learning effort strong. But he is also alert to the working of motivational factors and to those indications of motivational inadequacies in his teaching approaches. For this purpose it is useful to raise such questions as these repeatedly along the way:

- Does the trainee know what is expected of him?
- Are his points of view taken into account?
- Does he know the shape that learning is likely to take in his particular job?
- Is he receiving enough instructional attention?
- Is there adequate reinforcement for him in our teaching arrangements and techniques? Is there adequate feedback concerning progress?

In summary, a diagnostic look at the trainee's difficulties would center on specific indications:

- Errors in motion pattern
- Slowness of execution

- Inefficient use of perceptual feedback
- Difficulties with simultaneous motions
- Difficulties in the transitions between tasks or subtasks
- Difficulties with job organization and conflicting demands
- View of major job objectives as conflicting
- Difficulty in coping with changed job conditions
- Poor motivation.

Of course, the reason for diagnosing the learning difficulty is to arrive at specific and pertinent means of improvement. Such means are discussed in detail in Chapter 9 in connection with the progressive development of skill. The short listing of remedial actions below is intended to illustrate the differences among actions related to different causes and to suggest that a poor diagnosis or no diagnosis at all will lead to misdirected and wasteful efforts.

Remedying Learning Problems

Source of Problem	*Suggested Action*
If a simple method problem—	Regular coaching; possibly break job into smaller tasks.
If a simple speed problem—	Use pacing. For sustained effort, use rest periods and intermittent reinforcement.
If a perceptual problem—	Concentrate on quickest feedback signals; arrange the use of the most efficient channel; build confidence in such use.
If simultaneous motions are not used—	Go to a different feedback channel on one of the subtasks.
If bridging between subtasks is a problem—	Use anticipatory cues.

If job organization is a problem—	Review job schedule and priorities; coach in job routine.
If quality requirements are a restraining influence—	Practice with second-quality material until confidence in method is achieved.
If unusual conditions are a problem—	Define and review the conditions and the action to be taken under each; coach in actual situation or by simulation.
If motivation is a problem—	Consider consultation, transmittal of more information, more reinforcement.

Poor Performance Not Related to Learning Causes

It would be foolish to assume that all performance problems are learning problems, although as a practical course we must, as trainers, do what we can to stimulate learning under whatever conditions we face.

Performance problems arising early in the learning period are likely to respond to our training approaches and their motivational components. An exception occurs in a job which is so engineered as to require the performance of simultaneous subtasks (one subtask "internal" to the other) which because of human limitations cannot be executed at the same time. Later in the game the nonlearning obstacles to performance seem to increase. The output standards, for example, may require a pace which cannot reasonably be sustained. Or inadequate rest periods may be allowed. In addition, the employee may encounter job conditions which prevent him from organizing the job satisfactorily; some jobs have such variable and often unpredictable conditions—involving machinery and materials—as to make the job virtually unmanageable for even the most highly skilled employees.

Assuming that the trainee has developed job competence and the job is manageable, poor performance can then accurately be related to motivation. In such a case, the use of rewards and the employee's perception of what is rewarding in the job need to be examined.[1]

Finally, the lack of aptitude can influence performance unfavorably at early and late stages of learning. It should be kept in mind that the particular abilities associated with learning may be different from one stage of learning to another and that early success may not be a sure indication of the presence of aptitudes required for ultimate competence in the whole job.

STATEMENTS FOR DISCUSSION

The following statements raise for discussion the basic questions of the validity and usefulness of various "measures" of progress. They are statements from supervisors concerning the judging or measuring of the progress of trainees. Do you agree or disagree? Why?

1. It doesn't take me long to size things up. I can spot how a trainee is doing just in passing. It's no big deal. You don't have to watch him go through all the parts of the job. You can be sure that if he's fouling up on one of the tasks he's fouling up on all the others. You don't have to stand around to look at everything.

2. I don't bother checking anything during the first few weeks except for quality. If a trainee turns out good work, you know he's coming along all right. He will pick up all the rest.

3. All the little niceties of statistical measurement are fine, but we're running a business. You just need to get a general impression of the trainee. If the trainee is worth his salt he'll take it from there. Let him worry about the specifics once you let him know where his general faults lie.

4. A patient worker is a good worker. That's my motto. I like a trainee who takes his time—slow but sure, as the old saying goes. When I rate an employee I go to that aspect of his performance first. If I find him okay in that, I can trust him to be okay pretty much all the way down the line, on all other aspects of the job.

But watch out for those trainees who start out like a house afire. Those are the kind you've got to spend some time checking out.

---

[1]See Robert F. Mager and Peter Pipe, ANALYZING PERFORMANCE PROBLEMS, OR 'YOU REALLY OUGHTA WANNA' (Belmont, Calif.: Fearon Publishers, 1970), for a useful discussion of major causes of poor performance and a procedure for identifying and addressing them.

There's always something slighted or left out with that kind of worker.

5. The stop watch is the instructor's best friend. It tells the story of learning; it puts a finger on the progress of the trainee; it's right out there in black and white; it's the best measuring instrument in any training program. And if it is to give you the whole story of a trainee's progress, it has got to be used from the very beginning. Naturally, you have to show a trainee how to perform the task. But right after that the best thing to do is to reach for the old watch.

6. When I train a repairman I rely on one sure-fire indicator of competence. I just inspect his tool box. If it's neat and orderly with everything in its place and handy to get at, then I know he's doing a good job. If it's all jumbled up like a pile of scrap metal, I know I can't trust the man to keep my machines in running order. Yes, the tool box is a sure sign, a dead giveaway. If a mechanic can't keep that in order, he can't keep my machines in order.

7. When you refer to a valid measure of the progress of a piece-rate worker, of course you're talking about output figures. The story of the trainee's progress lies in his efficiency or output record. You don't have to look any further to tell what his successes are—and his difficulties, too. That's the whole story. That's all I need to know about him to push him ahead, and that's all he needs, too.

8. I can tell if the trainee is really coming along by asking him how many things he is checking as he works through the job task. I ask him, "How are you sure you're doing it right?" I do this at various points in the task. And if he can point to this and that, I know he's learning. The more checks he makes as he goes along and the more time he takes to make the checks, the better off he is. And the better his progress in learning the job.

Chapter 11

Conducting Discussions of Progress

Discussions of progress are important throughout the training period but never more so than at a late stage of learning, at the point when the employee's mastery of the full job is still in the balance. During this period he may need help in overcoming certain difficulties blocking the way as he moves to job competency and, at the last, in getting over the final hurdles to standard or piece-rate production. Experience is only part of the answer. He needs the kind of diagnostic help that will organize and use his experience so as to lead him to genuine skill.

The major objective in discussions of progress at this stage is to come up with courses of action or remedial steps aimed at the specific weaknesses which are holding the trainee back or slowing him down. But a supervisor usually cannot arrive immediately at remedies with any genuine assurance that the real troubles are being treated and that he is carrying the trainee along with him in his attempts at correction. It is advisable that he work through a series of orderly steps to arrive at corrective action, and the beginning of this systematic process is a determination of where the trainee now stands.

Valid, reliable, and unbiased information on the trainee's performance (the sorts of measures we have been discussing) is the raw material with which a fruitful discussion usually must start. The more objective these indices, the better, because a move into discussion of specific weaknesses is best made against a background of performance data on which everyone—including the trainee—can agree. If the supervisor can point to efficiency data, quality records, or other clear indications of performance (even ratings, if well supported, will serve), the trainee is more likely to agree on this starting point and to move jointly and cooperatively with the supervisor to causes and corrections. That is, we start with a look at the results and get agreement on them first.

Along with evidences of performance there should be points of reference telling supervisor and trainee whether the performance is good, average, or poor. Agreement should be reached on such a pegging of performance. Curves of expectancy, showing the average performance of past (but recent) trainees, are often useful for this purpose.

The next step is to determine what specific aspects of the trainee's performance are contributing to whatever poor results are found. (Even if the results are satisfactory, the discussion can center on aspects which, if improved, will bring even better results.) In this matter the supervisor may seek the opinions of the trainee, but the supervisor himself is in much better position to identify weaknesses if his observations have been adequate. The trainee, although often aware of general areas of difficulty, is not often aware of the specific sources of his trouble. For example, he will be aware of poor efficiency or excessive rejects in most cases but will usually be less aware of his precise errors or exact segments or aspects of the job or task in which his difficulties lie. That is, he can see the symptoms but may not himself have the best vantage point for an exact view of the ailment.

Of course, to be of real help to the trainee in the diagnosis of troubles, the supervisor must have sufficient knowledge of the trainee's performance to refer to specifics—to tasks or subtasks causing difficulties; to precise methods errors or inefficient procedures or routines; to lack of understanding concerning various job requirements such as quality, safety, and waste control; to the aspects of the task performance itself—errors of commission or omission in motion pattern or inspection procedures—which prevent the fulfillment of such requirements; to failures to attend to (or ignorance of) certain signs or evidences of how the work is progressing; to slowness on certain tasks or subtasks; to difficulties in assigning priorities or making best use of his time when several job demands come to his attention at the same time or in quick succession, and so forth.

As is evident from this listing of sources of difficulties,

which is far from complete, a pinpointing of errors or aspects of performance in which difficulties are encountered will often point to the cause of the difficulties. Sources and causes run together; when we really get down to cases, the cause often stands revealed or can be exposed by just a little additional probing.

In the interview the supervisor should attempt to bring the trainee to an acceptance of sources and causes of difficulties, through the trainee's participation if he has insights into his specific troubles, but in any event by reference to those exact aspects of the trainee's performance that are identified by adequate observation. At this stage acceptance is crucial because the trainee is not likely to apply himself wholeheartedly to a cure unless he feels it is really aimed at what ails him.

The next step, of course, is to arrive at a course of action. It can take many forms, depending upon the precise nature of the difficulty. If methods are at fault in a certain task or subtask, additional coaching on the job or in a vestibule establishment might be indicated; pacing arrangements might be used to help the trainee develop speed; explanations and illustrations can be arranged if knowledge and understanding of job standards (quality, waste, and so forth) are lacking or insufficient; a concentration on feedback might be tried if more precision needs to be built into the employee's performance; coaching in the regular routine and with a full job load might serve to teach job planning and the setting of priorities if these are the problems. The trainee's agreement on the course of action or acceptance of it is a major condition for improvement of performance.

An equally important requirement is follow-up by the supervisor to assure that the action decided upon is actually taken. If the supervisor commits himself to certain moves, such as bringing a job instructor into the act, the failure to follow up properly will place the full burden of the correction on the trainee (probably by a trial-and-error method) and will probably also be harmful to the trainee's motivation to improve.

It is obvious that a diagnostic look at performance and a carrying-through to corrective action and follow-up are especially required during leveling-off periods when the trainee is in dire need of help.

In summary, the discussion of progress should proceed by the following steps (in the form of questions):

1. Did the supervisor stress results (review evidence of progress with the trainee)?
2. Did he and the trainee come to an agreement on what the results were and whether they were satisfactory or not?
3. Did he look for the specific nature of the weaknesses in job performance, for causes of poor results?
4. Did he and the trainee come to a meeting of minds on causes?
5. Did he provide for correction, settle on a plan of action?
6. Did the trainee agree on the plan of action or accept it?
7. Did the supervisor provide for follow-up beyond the interview?

These questions are suggested for use in evaluating the performance of supervisors in practice interviews. For such practice a series of role-playing situations is provided in the following pages.

CASES FOR ROLE PLAYING

In Case 1 training needs become apparent, but they are not likely to be uncovered completely if the trainee himself is not heard. The third interview step—identifying specific weaknesses and their causes—is the crucial one in this case. A premature conclusion that the relationship between the operator and his repairman is at the heart of the problem will send the supervisor galloping after nebulous cures. This relationship will probably clear itself up if the operator improves in those aspects of job performance where he and the repairman rub.

In Case 2, the employee's perception is the key to the problem. The inadequate recent performance is not related to deficiencies in skill and will probably not be turned around by training efforts.

In Case 3, the learning itself does not appear to be as much of a problem as the employee's readiness to learn under training arrangements which are new to his experience and his acceptance of other job requirements. A reorientation in his thinking is a major objective of the interview. A plan of action and adequate follow-up on the job itself are also critical.

In Case 4, a diagnostic approach is clearly required—and a realization by the supervisor that the trainee's needs may change from one learning stage to another. An unvarying, all-purpose technique will not serve.

Case 1

Supervisor

I'll have to do something about Joe Smith's quality. I understand the problems a new man has—he's only been on the machine job two months. But he's turning out too many seconds. All kinds of defects are showing up from his machines.

He's a hard worker and he gets fairly good efficiency for a learner. But I've never seen a man on the move so much. He runs from pillar to post. But what he accomplishes is questionable—it's not quality, that's for sure.

If he's getting production without quality, I'd say this was his problem: He's running the machines when he should be stopping them and calling the troubles to the attention of the repairman. I've observed this about his work.

Of course, I've got my doubts about the repairman. He's a good mechanic when he wants to be. But he's not the most cooperative fellow in the world.

Summary of Joe Smith's Performance

Output record: Good, making piece-rate after only two months on job. The average time is about three months.

Quality: Not satisfactory. Ran 8% seconds last week, 9% week before. The average for trainees with his experience: 5% for these same periods.

Rating of performance on job tasks (rating by supervisor at end of past week):

Job Tasks	Method	Speed	Comment
1. Feeding stock into machine	Good	Good	
2. Setting and adjusting machine	Good	Fair	Seems to take too much time
3. Taking off finished pieces	Good	Good	
4. Making preventive maintenance checks on machinery	Fair	Fair	Seems haphazard

General comment: Smith spends too much time at one machine when others need attention. Doesn't seem to know what to do first.

Employee

I'm Joe Smith, a new machine operator. Well, not so new. I've been here two months and I've been assigned to a full workload of machines.

I've had enough training in most things. I know what to do. But there's one thing I don't have time to do, and that's making the maintenance checks—you know, getting around so I can spot trouble in advance or catch it before it happens or right when it happens. If anything is wrong on a machine, I'll catch it only if I happen to glance at the right place as I'm running by to do something else.

I wish the repairman would really fix these machines. I start one and in five minutes it's stopped again. So I start it again. And so on. If I call it to the repairman's attention, he sometimes seems to get mad at me about it.

I'm having trouble with quality. I guess it's because I don't have enough time to look at what's coming off the machines. But even if I get time to look—which is not very often—I'm not so sure what to look for. I've had a lot of defective pieces shown up to me, but don't have a full idea of the various kinds of defects I'm responsible for.

Case 2

Supervisor

John Jeffries is a puzzle to me. He's been making good progress as a stock handler, taking finished material off the machines, at least up to week ago. Now he's behind the job and doesn't seem to want to catch up.

He's a good boy. A recent high school graduate and a good mechanical prospect, and he seemed willing to try. I told him when I hired him that we'd keep him in mind for mechanical work. But what some of these new men don't seem to understand is that they've got to prove themselves on the first job before we can seriously think of moving them. They get awfully impatient.

I was hoping that Jeffries would be different. For the first five weeks I was still hoping. But last week—well, I don't know.

I wish the new men had the patience of some of the old ones. Like Henry Griggs, who stuck it out for years as a stock handler until a repairman opening came up—just last week. He'd filled in off and on, so he could step right into the repair job when it came open.

Summary of Jeffries' Performance

Output record: Good. Almost at piece-work rate of output after only six weeks on job. Average time taken to reach piece-rate output: eight weeks.

Rating of performance on job tasks (by supervisor at end of last week): Job methods: Good.   Speed: Poor

Comment: Jeffries has good methods and, up to this week, had good speed. Seems to be goofing off lately.

Employee

Boy, they can give this stock handling job back to the employment office if they will take it. I'm John Jeffries and I've tried to run this job, but it's too much for me.

I promised the employment man and the supervisor that I'd give it a try. Well, I've been on it for a month and a half, and I'm convinced this is not for me. I told the supervisor that I thought I could do something better (I'm a high school graduate) when I took this job, and he seemed to agree. He told me to stick it out if I could and he'd keep me in mind for other jobs if they came open.

I believed him, but a repairman job came open last week and they gave it to an older stock handler, Henry Griggs. I guess he deserved it; he'd been filling in as a repairman for years. But I could handle it if they gave it to me. I have good mechanical ability; the employment man told me so. But they didn't say a word to me when this repairman job came open.

The stock handling job is for the birds.

Case 3

Supervisor

I've been reviewing the progress of a new machine operator, Henry Jones, with our instructor—he's had him for a week—and a couple of things seem to be hindering Jones.

The instructor says Jones seems bright enough but that he wants to do things his own way and thinks he can do things much better than he actually can. Apparently Jones has had simple jobs before we hired him and has been left to learn them pretty much on his own.

He's having trouble especially with keeping things straight. We run different stock from time to time, and each type requires a little different handling—different machine set-up and varying machine operations. On other routine parts of the job he's doing all right. But if there's a change in stock, he may get started off all wrong.

One other thing. The instructor says Jones seems to think he can stop and talk as often as the experienced people. Apparently he doesn't understand that they may have their jobs caught up, while we're trying to make the most use of his training time.

I have called him to the office to discuss his progress. Next week we intend to continue keeping him with the instructor, working about the instructor's machines and concentrating on his weaknesses.

Instructor's Rating of Jones' Performance on Job Tasks

Job Task	Method	Speed	Comment
1. Start and stop machine	Fair	Good	Doesn't always check to see that everything is in order for starting.
2. Feed machine	Fair	Good	
3. Take off finished stock	Fair	Good	
4. Setting up machine for stock changes	Poor	Good	Can't seem to catch on to variations in set-ups.

General comment: Jones is fast, perhaps too much so. He seems to do things before thinking about what he's doing. He also tends to take breaks when he should concentrate on learning.

Employee

I'm Henry Jones, a learner on the machine operating job. I've been on this job for a full week now. I was with an instructor all the week learning how to feed the machine, remove the stock, and make changes in machine set-up when they change the stock. Those changes will kill you; they're hard as the devil to catch on to.

I say I was learning. What I meant was I was learning the instructor's way of doing things. Next week, I understand, I'm supposed to stay with the instructor again.

I guess there's a reason for this way of training, but I wish they'd just let me go ahead and run the machines. I notice some of the experienced operators, and it doesn't seem too hard to run this job. They even seem to have time to loaf around—you know, take a smoke or talk with the repairman. But when I have a little talk with someone, like the operators do, the instructor gets on me about it.

I've always learned things in my own way. I admit I've never run a job as complicated as this one, but I'd catch on to it better if I could learn it in my own way and do things the way that comes easy to me.

Case 4

Supervisor

Henrietta Brown has been on the assembly job for eight weeks. It's a complicated job and she's young. This is her first job, in fact. She started off very well, but for the last four weeks she has been producing far below what we expect of a trainee.

When she first fell off the pace (in the fifth week), we had the instructor work with her for a few hours on three consecutive days. She seemed to improve somewhat.

When she fell down on the seventh week we tried the same thing, letting an instructor work with her a few hours a day for several days. This time it didn't work. Now we're at the beginning of the ninth week, and I've got to talk with her.

I don't really know the trouble. Her methods are good. The ratings on that point, made out for last week, show that she follows correct methods on all the tasks of the job. And I find no fault with her quality, and that is crucial in this department and particularly so in her operation. We've got an inspection station right after her operation.

Employee

I'm Henrietta Brown. This is my first job. I'm on the assembly job and I'm having my problems. For the first couple of weeks I was doing fine, but from the fourth week on I've been having trouble. After the fifth week they put the instructor back with me (couple of hours a day for three days), and I improved some. But after the seventh week (another poor week) they tried it again, but I didn't improve much.

I don't know about this job. It's tougher than most other jobs here. I know how to do it but I just don't seem to get much production. Just slow, I guess. And I'm so worried about quality. It's emphasized so much; they test these assemblies right and left after I'm finished with them. A lot of parts have to go together and go together right, too, on my job. I'm just afraid to let myself go.

The instructor has been a lot of help, but I'm not so sure we've been working on my exact problem. I'm not so sure I know the problem. All I know is that I tend to be slow, and I'm afraid of turning out poor work.

Maybe this isn't the job for me.

Chapter 12

Motivation

Motivation is an important consideration in learning, and it would be misleading to discuss its role by treating it as an isolated phenomenon or in terms of unique techniques or procedures separate from the learning process itself. Learning and motivation are closely intertwined. It is basic to learning that the trainee be motivated, that is, stirred to activity and effort and pointed toward goals. Incidental learning—or learning at a low motivational level—does occur, but it is not usually the comprehensive sort of learning that the development of a high degree of job skill requires.

The intimate connection between motivation and learning is evident in the matter of reinforcement. If we genuinely reward the learner's responses in some way (by letting him know he is right or by recognizing or praising him for being right, for example), we apparently increase the probability that he will repeat those responses. It is also rewarding to the trainee to engage in activities which particularly please or interest him; the opportunity for such activities may be a practical reinforcer in certain jobs. In a job which includes several tasks of differing appeal to the trainee, the supervisor may find it possible to schedule the pleasing tasks after the others and to make the move to the pleasing tasks contingent on a certain level of performance in the less appealing tasks. Whatever the reinforcers, they can be an effective instructional tool; responses can be stamped in, shaped, and refined by them. They are at the heart of the learning process.

Of course, reinforcement is essential to the maintenance of behaviors after they are learned, but reinforcers are probably more easily applied and their effects more readily apparent in the learning process. The "menu" of reinforcers in the learning period need not be long: Information on good results, approval, praise, and recognition will serve the instructional purpose. And the schedule of reinforcement need not be complex—consistent reinforcement until the responses are fairly well set and errors eliminated, then intermittent reinforcement for the rest of the training period.

In animal learning, the responses are extinguished if the rewards (usually food) are withdrawn. But with human beings we can firmly establish the responses by means of reinforcement with some assurance that the responses, especially if they have begun to take on the strength of habit, will continue to be used when the immediate rewards are withdrawn. They will continue, that is, if the "larger" satisfactions available in the job make it worth the trainee's while. Although the beginning phase of learning can be heavily influenced by the reinforcement which an instructor or supervisor might provide, the extension of the effort so vital to the trainee's progress toward higher job skill cannot be assured unless the job provides some of the "larger" satisfactions.

In our training efforts we assume, though sometimes mistakenly, that we can build learning upon a base of motivation represented by the job itself. That is, we assume that the job offers or promises to offer something that the employee wants or needs—security, social satisfaction, achievement, or whatever. If we are right, there is a good chance that the learning will move forward. But even if we are right, we cannot always predict how far on the way to job skill or optimal job performance the basic need will carry the trainee. It depends, apparently, upon what the job means to the trainee—on the particular needs the job is regarded as fulfilling. Recent motivational studies have suggested, for example, that the need for economic security as a motive may push the trainee along to acceptable job performance, to the level of performance which will permit him to fill the minimum requirements of the job and thus remain employed. But perhaps no further.

If we want a higher level of performance (accompanied, by inference at least, by a greater development of skill), supposedly the very nature of the job must appeal to the trainee. Moreover, the job apparently should be seen by the employee as using his best talents and providing him with a sense of achievement and personal advancement.

Although the evidence is not yet conclusive as to the relative influence of specific job satisfactions or groups of satisfactions on performance, it is somewhat clear that an individual employee's efforts—and with them, his progress toward skilled performance—will depend upon (1) the importance to him of the satisfactions which good performance will provide and (2) the extent of the connection he sees between his performance and these important satisfactions. Obviously, if he perceives his efforts as eliciting no rewards or if the rewards are of little value to him, his effort will diminish.

Another influence on his effort is his expectancy in regard to achieving a "rewardable" level of performance, that is, his sizing-up of his chance of success. The effort tends to flag if he sees success as coming too easily or if—and this is the more common occurrence with young and inexperienced employees—he has little hope of "making it."

Not surprisingly, there are indications that motivation is increased if success is expected of the trainee. The supervisor and instructor should therefore communicate to the trainee through manner, speech, facial expression, and general demeanor that they are expecting the learner to succeed. On the other hand, if they give him the impression that they have little or no confidence in him and expect him to fail, failure becomes more of a possibility.

Of course, our mere expectation of success from the trainee or the trainee's own expectation of success will not assure the success. The assurance will come primarily through effective training arrangements and solid instruction of a sort which will translate the expectation of success into the experience of success (a stronger influence, still), specifically through such steps as breaking the job into tasks the trainee can learn quickly and by giving the direct coaching which can expedite the early development of skill.

Beyond the feedback and reinforcement given to the trainee as he practices the tasks in the early stages of his learning, we should, of course, continue to inform the trainee of his progress throughout the period of his skill-development. Such knowledge of results at the later stages will refer to larger goals of efficiency, output, and quality; and it should be given at appropriate intervals—when such operational data are still fresh and can be related to aspects of the employee's performance.

Information itself can have a motivational value since there exists in people a fundamental need to know and understand, to find out about things, to satisfy their curiosity. For this reason, aside from the rewarding value of knowledge of good results, it is advisable to inform the trainee concerning various aspects of his employment, his job, and his training as a continuous activity throughout the learning period.

The setting of goals is a much used procedure and should have a favorable effect if the goals are wisely set. That is, they should be definite challenges but not impossible for the individual in question to attain. And they will tend to exert a stronger pull on performance if the individual trainee has a say in setting them rather than having them imposed on him. Nevertheless, a reasonable goal, even if imposed, is probably better than no goal at all.

Of course, a goal must be repeatedly updated; for this reason goal-setting fits well into the system of periodic discussions of progress. Even at the very early stages of training, before evidence of progress shows up very definitely on the large indices of efficiency or quality, minor short-term goals can be used to advantage (such as a certain number of successive cycles of the task performed without error or at a specified rate of speed).

The setting of specific goals has a more favorable effect on performance than the mere admonition to do better. It serves to direct the trainee's efforts. But the strictly motivational aspect of goal-setting appears to lie in the trainee's commitment to the goal.[1] If we can secure such commitment, the effort is more likely to be forthcoming. The commitment and thus the motivation may be influenced by permitting participation in the setting of goals (as suggested earlier), putting the goal within

---

[1]John P. Campbell, Marvin D. Dunnette, Edward E. Lawler, III, and Karl E. Weick, Jr., MANAGERIAL BEHAVIOR, PERFORMANCE, AND EFFECTIVENESS (New York: McGraw-Hill Book Company, 1970), pp. 377–378.

reach, securing agreement on the goal, and providing strong
enough rewards for its achievement.

Meaningfulness of the learning task can add to the trainee's motivation to learn, and we should build meaning into our
instruction through such steps as the use of understandable
terms, the teaching of meaningful units of the job, the stressing
of purposes, the explanation of the reasons for certain job requirements or job methods, the tying-in of the job with the
process flow and the shaping of the product.

Finally, the approval of other people—instructor, supervisor, other employees—is a need which, if satisfied, can assist the
learning process. Tension may aid learning, but to expose the
trainee to excessive tension and pressure (such as many naive
employees may experience on their first industrial job) can interfere with the orderly acquisition of skills and disrupt the job
performance. The better course is to reduce tension, to assist
the trainee to adjust to the department and the people around
him as quickly as possible, and to provide him with sympathetic
attention, particularly at the crucial stages of his learning—
early in the game as he takes the first steps and later when he
tries to put all the parts together and to run the full job.

Factors Influencing Turnover

Research studies of turnover have shown the influence on
employee stability of such factors as "role clarity," feedback of
information on progress, the trainee's expectations, and the
trainee's experience of satisfactions or rewards.[2] Experience indicates that these same factors also have an effect on the effort
and performance of trainees and, by inference at least, on their
learning.

A clear statement to the trainee of what we expect of him
(clarifying his role) and a clear indication to him of how well he
is fulfilling these requirements—most importantly, of his progress in acquiring job skills—are highly likely to have a favorable
motivational impact and are the kinds of activities, fortunately,
a supervisor or trainer can readily engage in. While this feed-

---

[2]Lyman W. Porter and Richard M. Steers, *Organizational, Work, and Personal Factors in Employee Turnover and Absenteeism*, PSYCHOLOGICAL BULLETIN, 1973, *80*, 151–176.

back on progress at periodic intervals is important (see Chapter 11), the more immediate feedback related to the minute activities of the trainee as he undertakes the job tasks is, as stated earlier, at the core of the learning process—especially the positive feedback referred to as reinforcement.

Training's Effect on Expectations and Rewards

Since the trainee's expectations and their fulfillment appear to bear so directly on his effort, we must take them into account if we are to exercise any significant influence on his effort. If he is to exert the effort and persist in it, he apparently must have two positive expectations: (1) that he can make it on the job, that is, meet the job requirements, and (2) that making it will bring him satisfactions or rewards of value to him.[3] These expectations must be met. What role can training play?

Training is directly concerned with the first expectation (and meeting it) and indirectly with the second. Informing the trainee of job requirements will have the effect of making his expectations of achievement realistic (he may on his own size up the job as too easy or too hard); informing him of how we plan to teach him will have a further influence—a favorable one if our arrangements are seen as adequate—on his expectations of mastering the job. And, of course, the way we conduct the training will have a strong and direct bearing on whether or not this expectation is met.

A naive trainee is often so overcome by the size of the ultimate workload that he gives up early in the game. He loses sight of the possibility of achieving job competence by addressing himself to a systematic, step-by-step process of acquiring skill. Our training arrangements should provide for a planned and orderly progression through intermediate goals, and we should make this procedure and its anticipated outcome clear to the trainee.

Another aspect of training which affects the trainee's motivation and job progress involves the job conditions encountered by the trainee. If, despite his best efforts under good

---

[3]For a motivational model emphasizing the role of expectancies, see Campbell *et al.*, op. cit., p. 347.

training arrangements, the job will not run because of poor operating conditions involving materials or machinery, his motivation will flag. If he is not faced with such conditions or not
alerted to them before being put on his own, he will not be prepared to cope with them and may feel that his training was both
inadequate and misleading. Failure to run the job for reasons
beyond his control can bring a quick end to the possibility of
achieving various satisfactions normally available on the job.
The adverse effect of poor running conditions argues for the
improvement of those conditions which can be improved practically and for the preparation of the trainee to cope with those
conditions which cannot be modified.

Since the job rewards are so dependent on job competence,
the training which is intended to develop job competence in the
trainee will provide a major means of securing the rewards and
enabling the trainee to meet his second expectation. If the trainee does not "make it," few satisfactions are available to him, and
even these are temporary. Skilled performance makes possible
job security and expected earnings as rewards in themselves
and all the related satisfactions which these can result in.

So the idea in training is to get along with it and to move
quickly, because the rewards tend to lose their motivational
force if delayed. This is particularly true in piece-rate jobs
which provide for a minimum guaranteed rate until the trainee's output produces earnings above the guarantee. In such
case, the prospect of high earnings in the future may not sustain the learning effort if the future is considered remote and
the intervening hurdles mountainous. Through the use of effective training arrangements and techniques we are in a better
position to help the trainee surmount the obstacles and bring
the future—and its rewards—nearer.

CASES FOR DISCUSSION

The discussion cases that follow are primarily concerned with the
various aspects of the use of information in the supervisor's attempt
to keep the trainee "motivated": What information? How much? In
what form? In relation to what goals?

In the role-playing case (Case 5), a previously successful way of introducing change in job method went amiss in a new situation. The case offers the supervisor an opportunity to discover why and to recognize again (what his experience should already have taught him) that situations are never exactly the same and that the manner in which a promising solution is carried out may tip the scale against him.

Case 1

A supervisor was having difficulty getting standard efficiency from several groups of machines on which relatively new operators had been placed. He collected data on efficiency for all three shifts on these particular groups and similar data for groups of the same type of machines in this department. He called the substandard operators into a meeting in which he carefully explained how the standard was established, showed by actual figures how the standard was met or surpassed in other groups of the same machines, and gave specific data on the efficiencies over an extended period on the machine groups operated by the below-standard operators. He then suggested that now that the operators knew the problem they should go back to their machines and try to increase their efficiency. All the evidence indicated to him that the lagging efficiency among these particular operators was not due to poor attitude or poor effort. After a two-week period the supervisor reviewed efficiency figures for these particular machine groups and discovered that efficiency had not risen.

Question: What other information should the supervisor have discussed with the below-standard operators? What other steps should he have taken?

Case 2

A new man, hired for a machine operating job, reported for work early on his first day and waited outside the supervisor's office. Through the partly open door, he heard the supervisor talking to another employee. The conversation went like this:

Supervisor: Joe, I've got a new man coming in today and I want you to get him started on the machine.

Joe: Okay. But how does he look to you?

Supervisor: All right, I guess. No worse than the others we've been hiring lately.

Joe: That bad, eh? They haven't been a very good lot and that's a fact.

Supervisor: Well, this one may be different. He probably won't make it, but let's give him a try anyway. Let's give it a whirl.

Joe: Okay, if you say so. But I'm afraid we won't be whirling very long.

Question: If you were the new employee, what effect would this conversation have on your attitude toward learning the new job? How would you as a supervisor have conducted this conversation with the instructor? What can be done now?

Case 3

Statement by one supervisor to another supervisor: "I've had a belly full of that motivational crud, you know, that stuff they feed us in the human relations classes. Like pat the employee on the back; praise his achievement even if it's so small you can't even see it; emphasize the things he's doing right even if he's mostly wrong; let him know where he stands; and so on and on. I tried that on that new man, and as a result I'll be looking for a replacement for him tomorrow. I'll bet my shirt on that. I could tell by the way he reacted. This motivational stuff just won't work."

Statement by the new employee, describing his training to another employee: "I don't know if I'll stick around this place any longer. One thing I can't stand is a two-faced supervisor, a fellow who speaks out of both sides of his mouth. He was training me on the job, you know, and everything was all sugar and candy. Every time I made a move or turned around it was 'fine' and 'good.' Everything I did was great, just great, according to him. And then at the end of the week he called me into his office for a 'review of progress,' he called it, and guess what. I just wasn't good in anything. My quality was bad, my efficiency was below par, and so on. Now let me ask you, how can I be so bad when I'm so good? What the devil am I supposed to believe? I'd rather work some place where I can believe what they tell me. Where they tell it straight."

Question: What went wrong in the supervisor's efforts to motivate this employee? Discuss how you might make better use of praise and information.

Case 4

A supervisor explained how he went about motivating his trainees: "I'm all for this business of setting goals. That should do the trick for you. Five years ago we averaged out how the trainees were doing and set up some learning curves to give the new trainees some week-to-week goals to shoot at. I've used these same curves ever since. And with success, I believe. At least up to now.

"What I've been doing for the last five years is to post the output figures for each trainee each week and plot them on display charts, against the curve. By name, too. And right out in the open so everyone could see.

"This idea has a lot of things going for it. There's a lot of motivation in setting up a curve as a continuing goal and posting figures for each trainee every week so he can see whether he's meeting the goal or not. So you have goals, and you are feeding information on progress to trainees, and by the public posting you add the social bit. That's a lot of motivation wrapped up in one package. That tells the story. You don't even have to talk to the trainees—and I don't—because they can see right there where they stand.

"Now recently I've had a couple of trainees who somehow haven't responded. They haven't gotten the message. I don't know why. Motivation is motivation. The posting ought to have jacked them up especially, because they stay pretty far behind the goals. But it hasn't yet, even after two months. They just don't want to work, I guess."

Question: What opinion do you have of this supervisor's arrangements for motivating trainees? Why, in your opinion, is the arrangement having no observable effect on the new trainees?

Case 5 (for role playing)

Supervisor (Don Edwards)

Just when you have a good thing going, something happens. I don't know exactly what in this case. It puzzles me.

When we changed the method on one of our jobs, we really laid it out on the table for the operators. We explained to them what the changes were and why we made them. (Mind you, a rate change was involved here, too.) We retrained each of the operators in a vestibule set-up and then followed up on the line to help the operators with any further difficulties. We really spent time with them. And it worked like a charm. Good output, no grievances, and no one greatly disturbed.

But the second operation, well, it was just the opposite. A disaster. Everyone upset. And, believe me, we followed exactly the same procedure as before: full information, a real training effort, continuous consultation with the employees. But it flopped. I noticed early in the game that a few of the employees were spending a lot of time off the job and, just out of curiosity, I timed their absences and kept a record of them. Things just went from bad to worse. After a while they were spending more time in the latrine and the smoking booths than on the job.

I thought I might get Mary Henry to talk some sense into the others. She's an old-timer in this second operation I'm having trouble with, and all the women respect her. She's always been loyal to the company. I've asked her to come in to see me.

Employee (Mary Henry)

I think I know what my supervisor, Mr. Edwards, wants. It must have to do with the methods change.

I've always liked working here; I've been here a long time. But this business we're now involved in has me disturbed. Really disturbed. Why don't they treat us like adults instead of children? When they started the methods improvement project, as they called it, on our operation, everything seemed to be working out just fine. They explained about the changes, what they were and why they made them and all. And they made a real effort to train us to do the job in the new way. But that soft-soap approach didn't last very long. Pretty soon Mr. Edwards was out there in the line acting like a policeman, timing how long we stayed in the toilet. Can you imagine that? We know this for a fact because one of the employees, Sue Sanford, saw the notes he wrote down on his clipboard. That tore it.

Chapter 13

Retraining of Experienced Employees

The retraining of experienced employees is a difficult and bothersome problem which a supervisor is often tempted to sweep behind the door and forget. Retraining is not a unitary problem which can be solved with a single and unvarying approach. This fact contributes to the difficulties of retraining, but, fortunately, gives clues as to the solutions as well. That is, if we can precisely define the problem of the moment and design our training to meet this specific problem, rather than placing reliance on the same broad approach each time, we have a much better chance of success.

Retraining activities may be classified as group training or individual training. Group training may arise as the result (1) of below-standard performance of a department or plant as a whole in such operating indices as quality, waste, or efficiency or (2) of major changes in job methods, machinery, equipment, and so forth affecting numbers of people. Individual retraining occurs primarily when a single employee is found to be operating below standard in a significant aspect of his job such as quality or output.

This classification has no merit except to introduce the idea of a specific approach no matter what the general nature of the problem or the name we apply to it. Group training should not take the same shape each time, without regard to the specific objective of the training. For example, group training of a type designed to reduce waste is unlikely to work if applied without modification to the problem of quality improvement (as we will attempt to illustrate). The problem and the training in both these cases will be concerned with a group of employees, but the effectiveness of the solution will depend to a large extent upon our perception of differences in the two situations. The same necessity for discrimination in approach is true of individual retraining; the approach must be geared to the needs of the individual.

Group Retraining

Example: Waste Reduction

As an illustration of group training, let us first discuss an actual group program in waste reduction. The need for such a program was evidenced by continuing production of waste above the percentages allowed in carefully set standards. This need was found in a number of processes; the problem was mill-wide. The approach used in the solution of the problem, a typical approach of a "participative" type, included the steps listed below. This procedure was taken with separate groups of employees, the composition of each group being determined by assignment to a common process or job classification.

1. Presentation of the problem by the mill superintendent and department foreman with particular reference to (1) money cost of waste, in specific detail, at the processing point at which these employees were involved and (2) the employees' own economic stake in waste reduction. This presentation was made in a group meeting of employees.
2. Soliciting of suggestions for reduction of waste from the employees at this same group meeting.
3. Individual interview with each employee at his workplace by a supervisor or a Training Department representative for the purpose of (1) further discussion of waste reduction, with direct reference to the employee's own work, and (2) further soliciting of suggestions.
4. Consideration of suggestions and determination of specific waste-reduction steps to be taken in the particular process.
5. Reporting back to each employee who made a suggestion concerning the disposition of the suggestion.
6. Presentation to employees, in group session, of the waste-reduction steps and suggestions to be adopted in this particular process. This was done by the department foreman.

7. Follow-up by the foreman, assistant foreman, and in some cases by repairmen to assure that the steps were being taken.

8. Posting of charted data in the department to show, week by week, the percentage of waste produced in the process as compared with the allowed standard.

9. Recognition of accomplishment through continued attention from department supervision, mill management, and in some instances from members of general company management. Additional recognition through articles in the employee paper.

As is evident from this list of steps, the approach was largely motivational in nature. No improvements in manipulative skill or significant changes in job methods were made. There was an attempt to clarify standards for judging whether certain types of waste were salvageable or not and to secure better segregation of the various types. But beyond this point, little of the usual kind of job training was done, and the resultant improvement in the waste index meant primarily that the employees simply conserved reworkable stock. In some jobs this meant literally picking it up from the floor.

The chief motivational procedures for employees in this program were: (1) participation by the employees in the solution of the problem, chiefly through the giving of suggestions; (2) knowledge of the results of their efforts; and (3) nonfinancial rewards in the form of attention and recognition.

The approach appeared to be eminently fitted to the problem, as evidenced by significant immediate improvement in most processes and significant long-term improvement in at least one process. Yet even in this latter case of enduring improvement, a modification or at least a strong reinforcement of the original approach was necessary in order to maintain the gains as time brought changes in the work situation and in the attitudes of employees. Apparently, one should not confidently anticipate long-term effects from largely short-term motivational programs. The motivational steps may have to be continued or re-introduced to maintain results if we are relying exclusively on them for job-performance improvements.

The one technique which is usually continued in motivational programs is the knowledge of results (ordinarily given in chart form). Experience with this technique as a follow-up device suggests that it is essential to continued improvement but in itself may not be enough to sustain or improve the gains as time goes on. At some point along the way, the effect of participating in the original establishment of the program is in danger of wearing off or wearing thin. If this basis is lost or weakened, the knowledge of results may come to be regarded as somewhat pointless. When an employee loses personal identification with the thing being measured, he is then unlikely to be influenced strongly by information on where he stands in it. If he does not basically care about the results, knowledge of them tends to make little difference to him. So, in a waste-control program, the weekly percentage figures may become a matter of indifference to the employee. Such an eventuality would suggest a need for further discussions and suggestion-seeking, at least on an individual basis, to reestablish the foundation of participation and personal attention.

Where changes in personnel occur, knowledge of results would be expected to have even less effect since the newcomers have had no personal involvement in the program. The first steps of the program, involving participation, should be repeated for them.

In summary, a motivational approach to an operational problem may bring about a short-term improvement but should not be expected to produce long-term results unless provisions are made both for (1) giving knowledge of results to employees and (2) taking supplementary steps for dealing with changes in the attitudes and composition of the workforce.

Further, a purely or largely motivational approach such as the one illustrated by the waste program, whether short-term or long-term, is not likely to bring maximum results if improvement of performance is dependent upon an increase in actual job skill or the development of new job skills. We will turn now to a problem whose solution is dependent on the job skills of employees.

Example: Quality Improvement

The approach outlined above is likely to prove less effective for a program aimed at improvement in quality than for a program of waste control. As supervisors know, there are factors influencing quality which motivation alone will never reach. We may motivate our employees to a point where they want to do everything in their power to reduce seconds. But, unfortunately, they cannot reduce seconds by occasionally picking something from the floor. Aside from considerations of machinery, equipment, materials, and other factors affecting quality which are beyond the control of the employees, we must establish in our employees those job skills which will result in the production of quality goods.

When poor or inappropriate job skills are a cause of poor performance, as is usually true in the matter of quality, knowledge of results is of little effect because it neither points to specific remedies nor provides for their application. It is not enough to tell employees how poor their record is. We must help them to find and use the means of improving it. Specifically, we must help them determine exactly what aspects of their job skills are causing trouble and must provide the kind of training required to imbed "quality ways" firmly into the structure of the revised skills. The intent to "get in there and fight" is fruitless unless we know what weapons to use against the enemy and how to use them.

Moreover, when changes or improvements in job skills are required, a strong or exclusive reliance on motivational techniques often leads to frustration. Motivation is important in any program of improvement, but in itself it will not teach an operator to perform the job tasks in such a way as to assure quality. If insufficient skill in the performance of job tasks is causing seconds, the obvious solution is the development of skill, undergirded by whatever motivational assists we can give to the employee but recognized as the heart of the matter.

A diagnostic analysis of job performance would be necessary, of course, to identify the specific causes for poor quality so that the appropriate attack can be made. Our only purpose at this point is to illustrate that the program must be pertinent to the problem; a bag full of all-purpose gimmicks will not serve for all purposes.

Changes in Manufacturing Processes and Job Methods

In those problems arising from major changes in job methods, processing procedures, machinery, equipment, or layout, a combination of motivational steps and skill training is usually appropriate. Both are important. A motivational or attitudinal approach is needed to help the employee adjust to change; skill training is needed to teach new job methods, operation of new equipment, and so forth. These approaches are interrelated, of course; if an employee resists a change in job method he is likely to make the sort of progress in learning (at least, as measured by performance) that is far short of his capabilities.

Normally, in changes of this sort the chief motivational means at the disposal of the supervisor is the giving of information. To be effective in influencing attitudes, however, the information apparently must be given in certain ways and under certain conditions.[1]

Here are some of the circumstances under which the giving of information by a supervisor seems to be most successful in bringing about attitudes conducive to relearning:

1. The information concerning the change should be given to the employee before the date of the change—the earlier the better. This early notice will enable the employees to prepare for the change. It also permits participation in some degree; the employees may themselves make useful suggestions concerning the change and its installation. There is danger, of course, that an adverse attitude will develop with early information, but generally the chances of a favorable (or least unfavorable) attitude are better with early information than with late.

2. All the employees involved in the change should receive the information.

3. The information should be thoroughly understood by the supervisor who gives it. He should have sufficient informa-

---

[1]See Theodore M. Newcomb, Ralph H. Turner, and Philip E. Converse, SOCIAL PSYCHOLOGY (New York: Holt, Rinehart and Winston, 1965), pp. 94–114, for discussion of influence of information on attitudes.

tion and should be seen as clearly more expert in the subject of the change than the employees under him.

4. The supervisor should have the firm conviction that the change is good for his department. He should identify himself with the change; it should be *his* change, not a change he feels is imposed upon him by higher management or by the Engineering Department or Industrial Engineering Department. (Such identification with the change would require participation by the supervisor himself in the planning of the change.)

5. The information should be understood by the employees. It should therefore be given in terms they understand, and a major emphasis should be placed on the reasons behind the change.

6. The supervisor should be perceived by the employees as carrying out an intent to inform rather than to "sell" them or give them a "snow job." His information should be regarded as unbiased.

7. If the supervisor's attitudes on other matters are regarded by the employees as generally agreeing with their own, he is in a stronger position to influence them in a specific instance of possible disagreement—over a job change, for example.

8. Finally, the supervisor who is considered as trustworthy and honest and has the respect of his employees will carry more weight, with the information he imparts, than the supervisor who is not so highly regarded.

In the installation of the change, the surrounding conditions should be carefully worked out to prevent hitches. For example, if the change involves job methods, the flow of materials and the condition of the materials and the employees' equipment should be good. Otherwise, the new job methods cannot be used in their full effectiveness, and any beginning resistance to the change by the employee is likely to continue or worsen. He will be more firmly convinced than ever that the change will not work. And he will tend to blame all irritating conditions on the new change and center all his gripes and complaints, from whatever source, on it. His resistance is thus confirmed.

In the retraining which accompanies major changes, then,

the suggested procedure is first to lay the groundwork for acceptance of change by giving information to employees and by setting up the physical conditions which will permit the change to work. Under these circumstances, retraining in job skills becomes more acceptable to employees. Relearning is still difficult for experienced employees, but a favorable attitude gives them a running start.

The techniques and arrangements proposed earlier for the training of new employees can be applied in considerable part to the retraining of experienced employees. The discussion of the transfer of skills is particularly pertinent since transfer is a major problem when job methods are changed. The unaided employee will tend to bring his earlier—and often inappropriate—skills into play. Hence we must give him the sort of guidance which will:

1. Specify the elements and principles which he can carry with him into the modified job. This step requires, as a basis, a careful analysis of job methods—the new compared to the old.

2. Provide him with adequate and guided practice in the new elements (and in the combination of appropriate old and new) until the reconstructed pattern of motions becomes the habitual pattern upon which he will rely in all circumstances—in emergency as well as routine situations.

Even small changes in job methods require persistent practice in order to establish them as part of a fixed pattern and to prevent a reversion to old methods. Explanation or demonstration or a combination of both does not usually provide sufficient prompting to assure that the employee, through the subsequent practice, will make satisfactory progress toward the required level of skill in the modified methods. The instructor should go beyond explanation and demonstration to give help to the employee in the actual doing, should coach him, that is, by cues and feedback as he starts practicing the revised tasks so as to give him a maximum boost toward skilled performance. Of course, he must go on his own. But in situations of change we tend to put an experienced employee on his own too soon and invite him thereby to wheel his old interfering habits into action. We need to start him off strongly in the practice of the new method and keep him under surveillance until the new method really "sets in."

Individual Retraining

When mechanical or processing changes occur, an analysis is required, as we have seen, to determine what changes in job method the trainee must make in order to adapt to the mechanical changes. Analysis is equally important and often more difficult in the case of an individual employee who, in an unchanged situation, fails to meet certain standards of job performance. We must, in the latter case, find out what the employee's specific difficulties are. But even before our analysis becomes specific—that is, genuinely diagnostic—we must find out if the employee's performance is really deficient or only seemingly so. Both these searches are simply a matter (though not simply done) of moving toward an identification of training needs.

The first question to resolve is the amount of trust which can be placed in the measure of performance which purportedly shows that the individual employee is operating below par. Most manufacturing departments, particularly those having piece-rate operations, use indices of performance which show individual output or efficiency. And in many instances a quality figure (in terms of the percentage of output which is defective) and a waste figure are also available. If we are to accept these figures as authentically representing the individual employee's performance, we must be sure that the indices meet the criteria discussed previously, that they be relevant, reliable, and unbiased measures. When subjective ratings are used as a measure of performance, the need to examine the measure is even more acute.

The employee's degree of control over what shows up on the index is an essential consideration. Let us take a machine operator as an example. Does the figure assigned to him on the index truly reflect what *he* has done or failed to do, how well or poorly *he* has performed the assigned tasks? In certain machine operating jobs the output figures are influenced as much by auxiliary employees (stock handlers, repairmen) as by the operator himself. Similarly, the quality figures are often as much the result of the repairman's maintenance work as the operator's actions. The work of the operators assigned to the same machines on other shifts also has an effect.

Another limitation on control is imposed by the condition of the materials and the basic condition of the machines and equipment (in addition to the effectiveness of routine repairs). If an operator encounters a run of poor stock or if he is stuck with a troublesome machine, his level of performance as shown on the index may be an erroneous statement of his competence. The effect of these abnormal and often temporary conditions must be taken into account before we conclude that such and such a production or quality figure for such and such a time indicates a need for retraining.

Another consideration is the standard itself which serves as the reference point by which we decide whether performance is good or poor. For each of the performance indices in use, a department will usually have such standards, based on machine stoppage studies, past records, and other operational data. The standard itself can be unrealistic, particularly if it is retained so long as to fail to reflect long-term changes in operating conditions. And it will be temporarily inappropriate in times of temporarily abnormal operating conditions.

Let us assume that we have leaped all of the hurdles to this point; our measures are true and our standards are reasonable. Can we then conclude that an operator who drops below the standard is a poor operator in need of help? Not necessarily. The crucial question is: How far below?

While a supervisor need not be a statistician to judge an employee's performance, he must realize there are chance fluctuations on any performance index. That is, an operator can fall a certain distance below standard simply on the basis of chance. The cause does not necessarily reside in the actual job performance of the employee. However, if the employee's position on the index falls a so-called "significant" distance below the norm, the effect of chance is not the compelling factor, and we must look into the various aspects of the employee's performance to get to causes. There is something genuinely to be concerned about in this instance.

A supervisor may have staff help to call upon to tell him what must be the size of the fluctuation in an operator's mark on the index in order to represent a significant change. In the absence of such information, the supervisor should guard against becoming excited over the very slight drops in the output or quality figures of an experienced employee whose performance has been meeting the standard. Minor fluctuations are inevitable and signify little or nothing. If the drop is substantial and it persists, the supervisor then knows that the employee is in trouble and that action is indicated; small changes of short duration are an insufficient basis for action-taking.

If the employee is found to be in genuine difficulties in regard to his actual job performance for reasons other than operating conditions, what specific action should the supervisor take? A diagnostic look at the operator's performance is certainly required. The indicated first step is the obvious one of examining the operator's performance in each of the job tasks or subtasks by (1) observing his methods for detection of error, (2) timing him to detect slowness of pace, and (3) questioning him to uncover weaknesses of understanding.

The findings during our observations often contradict the performance figures. The operator will be observed to be following correct methods and to be completing each task or subtask in standard time but still will not manage to achieve a daily or weekly standard of output. The customary gesture at this point is to cry "effort" on the assumption that the employee "knows what to do but won't push to do it."

Inadequate effort is indeed the answer in many cases. But without a really comprehensive look at job performance, a look at the finer aspects of performance beyond the basic motion pattern, it is a premature answer. As a premature answer it is often an erroneous answer which may lead to unjustified disciplinary actions against an employee—a punishing experience for the employee and a self-defeating procedure for the supervisor. The training objective is lost in the process and so—too often—is the employee.

There are subtle aspects of job performance which elude the stop watch and an observation of the more superficial points of job method. An employee can meet standard time on each subtask and perform each by "correct" method but not be able to bring the subtasks together as a coordinated, rhythmic whole. He may need help in bridging over quickly from one subtask to another, in picking up and interpreting the cues which will signal him through the transitions. There is a perceptual aspect to this process of building quick connections which the concentration of our observations on the employee's overt activity, subtask by subtask, may never uncover.

Or the employee may be making the right moves but using the wrong sensory channel to guide him through the task. He may still be relying on vision, for example, when a genuine advance in skill would require a shift to a reliance on "feel." He will be hard put to sustain speed in the total task if he is forced, because of inefficient feedback, to apply his efforts to those fragments of the tasks—the reaches and moves—which are least subject to improvement.

Or the employee may be having trouble with simultaneous or closely adjoining elements or subroutines. We may have to help him in those aspects of the job which place a heavy demand on the senses, in terms of requiring him either to pick up and act on signals appearing at very short intervals or to give attention to two subroutines at the same time.

Or, in a task consisting of a quick series of precise, short-cycle operations which build progressively to the final resolution of the task, the employee may now and then be forced into delays and hesitations which a short observation may not detect and an analyst trained strictly in motion patterns may not understand. The difficulty will have nothing to do with effort but will instead be occasioned by the employee's need to perceive how things are going, what is under control, and what lies ahead. In this particular sort of task, he cannot sustain the pace indefinitely but must pause now and again to size up where he stands. He does not need help on the motion pattern; he does not need the stop watch; he does not need to be pushed to greater effort. He needs to improve in the "sizing-up" process.

Or, in a job which involves the operation of a number of machines and the performance of various tasks at each machine, the employee may need help in "organizing" the job, in putting all the parts together through a system of schedules and priorities. He can be seen and measured as expert in the performance of each task but may still fail to "keep on top of" the total job.

In these instances, a concentration on effort is a misdirection; it is likely to compound the problem.

In many cases effort is the employee's means of compensating for lack of skill or for slowly developing skill in such critical aspects of performance as we have described above. The employee may use excessive effort on those performance aspects already under his control, and by such effort he may succeed in meeting the output norm. But he is likely to be over-extending himself; the effort, restricted to the simpler elements of the job, may not be an adequate way of sustaining his output level over the long-run. Such effort may put him up there but is unlikely to keep him there for long; it is not a stout enough perch.

If he applies a heightened effort, expressed through speed, to his areas of weakness, he often finds that he is defeating his purpose. The links in his chain of motions, tenuous as they are, may be loosened as he makes his helter-skelter gallop through. His total performance may suffer. Eventually he may clear up his weaknesses, but the clearing-up can be accomplished more quickly and much less painfully if we give him the indicated kind of training assistance.

If an employee is left to his own devices, a major weakness may never be overcome in certain instances. Sewing is a case in point. In towel hemming, the procedure, representing a high order of skill, requires the operator to reach and pre-position the second edge of the towel while hemming the first end. Some operators never manage to master these routines as simultaneous operations. After many years of experience on the job, they continue to delay the reach until they finish the hemming. In order to meet the standards they must concentrate heavily on the reach, but the maximum possible gain in speed in this element is narrowly limited. Unless they learn to complete the reach "internal" to the sewing, they must "knock them-

154

selves out" in order to make the rate. And they usually fail to make it consistently. They need help.

Genuine training approaches, then, are required in the retraining of experienced employees. But in order to assure that our training approaches themselves are not misdirected, we need to take a very close look at the employee's performance, the sort of perceptive, diagnostic look which will uncover real difficulties.

Our major intent in this discussion of individual retraining is to emphasize the importance of an adequate determination of training needs when we are dealing with below-par performers among experienced employees. The training steps to be taken to meet the various needs have been previously suggested in Chapter 9 in connection with our discussion of the later stages of learning; they need not be repeated here.

The preoccupation with retraining in this chapter is not an advocacy of training as the exclusive response to performance problems; the employee may indeed have other needs. But neither must we understate the need for training. The point is this: We should not dismiss training as an answer until we have taken a close look at the employee's skill—its state and its components —to determine if it is a sufficient underfooting for sustained performance at an adequate level.

Training of Newly Hired Employees With Experience

The determination of training needs is a critical procedure in the case of a new employee who claims to have had experience elsewhere in the sort of job in which we are placing him. We cannot afford to gamble on the pertinence of that experience to the skill requirements of our particular job. We must retrain the employee. And as the first step in the training we must thoroughly analyze his performance, in line with the diagnostic points previously discussed, to determine what his specific training needs are. Then, of course, we must take action to meet these needs, to arrange to give the required help rather than to rely upon the new employee to modify or improve his job skills by his own largely trial-and-error efforts.

CASES FOR DISCUSSION

The following discussion cases are concerned with such matters as the method of retraining, introduction of changes requiring new learning, use of instructor, and whether training is needed.

In the first role-playing case (Case 8), the supervisor is given an opportunity to discover how a simple change in job method can pose a difficult (perhaps impossible) learning task. The second role-playing case (Case 9) reveals the adverse consequences of a misjudgment of an experienced employee's problem. In Case 10, the supervisor's effort to improve performance runs against an employee's firmly established concept of standards of performance. In the last role-playing case (Case 11), a major change in job structure results in several problems in regard to motivation and learning. In it the supervisor must uncover a training need which he assumed had already been met.

Case 1

A technician from a machinery manufacturing company was sent into a department to supervise the installation of new machinery purchased from his company. The departmental supervisor arranged to have him train the three operators who were to be transferred to the new machines from older models of the machines.

The technician gathered the operators around him and carefully explained and demonstrated the several tasks of the job. Then he stopped.

The supervisor, who had been observing the instruction, said to the technician, "That was a good start. When can you get back to work some more with these operators?"

The technician appeared somewhat surprised. "I don't understand," he said. "I've already taught them what to do."

Question: Had the technician "taught" them? What would you advise the supervisor to do?

Case 2

A supervisor explained how his retraining plans went awry.

"I thought I had the training problem on the new machines licked. My plan was a good one. I planned to use my best operator on the older machines as my instructor. And I had one of the new machines set up in a vestibule room as a training machine. The idea was to train the instructor first and then have him train the other operators and feed them into the department as the new machines were installed.

"This old operator I selected to be my instructor was my best operator. A real whiz. And he had had more experience on the old machines than any man in the department. If anyone could learn the new machines in a hurry, he was the one.

But, do you know, he had a devil of a time with the new machine. I finally gave up on him, and in desperation—just because he was available—I turned to my greenest operator to see if he could help us out. He had been on the operator job only two weeks and was about to be laid off because with the new machines turning out so much work we would need one less operator. He was it.

"Boy, did he surprise me! He took off like a flash. Oh, he had a little trouble with the new machine, but very little. And imagine, that fellow hadn't even learned how to operate the old machine yet."

Question: What explanation would you give to this supervisor? For the differences in success between the two operators? For the difficulties encountered by the experienced operator?

Case 3

A new supervisor prided himself on the close watch he kept on the piece-rate earnings of the employees in his department. He kept a day-by-day record of their production and earnings. If an employee's output dropped even slightly below the expected piece-rate level on a particular day, he would be right there with the employee the next day to "nose out the difficulty," as he expressed it.

The only trouble with this arrangement was that in many cases it didn't seem to work. Here's how the supervisor described one instance of failure.

"On Tuesday this operator—an experienced man—fell two percentage points below his piece-rate quota. He usually produced right at the mark or a little higher. So naturally I got right into the problem on Wednesday. I made a thorough check on this man's methods; I even timed him on a few tasks. But in spite of my best efforts I couldn't spot where he was falling down. I even had one of our industrial engineers check him out, and he couldn't find anything wrong with his performance, either. We'll have to look again tomorrow— Thursday, that is. We just haven't spotted the weakness, but it's bound to be there."

Question: Was a weakness "bound" to be there? What would you have the supervisor search for? Would you have him search at all?

Case 4

On a machine loading job, the method was revised in the interest of greater efficiency. Instead of handling five pieces of stock at a time, the employees were now to handle only three at a time. The five-at-a-time method of loading had the appearance of being faster, but the amount of fumbling with the five pieces was found to offset the advantage of handling the greater number of pieces. A thorough investigation established the superiority of the three-at-a-time method. It was definitely faster.

The supervisor assumed that if an employee was accustomed to handling five at a time, the handling of a reduced number would be an easy matter. But he decided to make a real effort at retraining. His training consisted largely of an explanation and demonstration of the new method and a few cycles of practice for each employee. The training seemed to go well.

The next day the supervisor made the rounds of the department, confidently expecting to see his employees performing the loading job by the new method. The first employee he observed, an experienced stock handler, was using the old five-at-a-time method. When the supervisor asked why, the employee replied, "I just got behind, and I just had to do something to catch up so these machines wouldn't run out of stock."

Question: What could have been done to keep the employee from reverting to the old method? Did the supervisor size up his training problem correctly? Explain.

Case 5

A supervisor described his experience in training his machine operators to use a new attachment.

"I bought this new attachment for the machines because it was a real help in guiding material into the machine. By the old arrangement the operator did the guiding by hand, and that was a job of maneuvering, let me tell you. With the attachment, you just flipped it into position, aligned the material along its edge, and off you went. The attachment did most of the work.

"I saw this gadget as a real advantage for the operators, and the beauty of it was that practically no training would be required. One demonstration would do it.

"But I didn't want to get the operators all upset over the change. You know how they worry about things. You tell them something is coming up, and it really upsets them. So the most reasonable thing to do was to install the attachments on the machines over the weekend and then just start the operators off with the new attachments on Monday. Sweet and simple. No fuss and bother.

"Well, that's what I did. And, frankly, it was no go. Just another good idea that got sabotaged. My operators took a dim view of the whole idea. Some of them used the attachment pretty well; some others suffered a drop in production; and, you won't believe this, two of my operators tore the attachment off the machine and went back to the old hand-guiding method. I'll have to take disciplinary action against those two.

"Where did I go wrong?"

Question: Where did this supervisor go wrong? What should he do now? Did you agree with his way of introducing the change?

Case 6

New and improved models of machines were to be installed in this supervisor's department. He had a definite approach to his retraining problem. He explained how he planned to proceed.

"My operators are all experienced people and proud of wnat they can do. You've got to take that into account when you consider how to introduce new machines to them. You can't treat them like inexperienced kids who never saw a machine before. You can't spoon-feed them.

"What I plan to do about training my operators on the new machines is simply this. I'll tell them exactly how they've got to change their job methods in order to run the new machines. There are differences. Then I'll show them a film we've made of an operator performing the job tasks on the new machine, using the right methods. It's a film we made at one of our other plants where we installed the new machines some months ago. Then I'll leave it up to them. As I say, they are all experienced machine operators. They'll take it from there.

"Incidentally, I've seen the film and it's great. As they say, a picture is worth a thousand words. And this film is worth a half dozen instructors."

Question: What is your opinion of this supervisor's plans for retraining his operators? What suggestions would you make to this supervisor concerning the use of his job-method film?

Case 7

A supervisor explained how he relied on his experienced employees to handle small changes in job methods: "When you have to retrain really experienced people after a job-method change or change in equipment, you usually don't need to go very far with your training. Maybe you do if the change is a big one. But not if the change is minor. You can forget the demonstration. They don't need it. I just call them into the office as a group and tell them what to do. Forget the old way and do it such and so from now on, that's what I tell them. That's all they need. Besides, how would I demonstrate? I don't have any skill in doing the things in the new way. I can tell them how it's to be done, but the doing is up to them."

Question: How far do you think this supervisor should go in retraining for small changes?

Case 8 (for role playing)

Supervisor (Tom Hankins)

It was a simple matter. Instead of attaching the label at the top of the item, as one of the first steps in processing the item, the Sales Department requested that the label be placed about halfway down the item. At that position, the label would be visible in a new package Sales had designed to show off the product. As I say, a simple matter. Why the operators had trouble I'll never know. When I set up the new procedure, calling for the label in the middle, the operators dropped dead on me. No one has made the rate yet, and we started the new set-up a week ago. I've got to get to the bottom of this. I'll start by questioning Homer Jenks, one of my most reliable men. But even he's fallen down on me.

Employee (Homer Jenks)

The Sales Department and the supervisor, Tom Hankins, ought to have their heads examined. Nothing to it, Hankins said. A simple request from the Sales Department, he said. Boy, I'd like to see them try making that item with the label in the middle. Before, all we had to do was start the item into the machine, attach the label right then, and off we'd go, full speed ahead. Attaching the label didn't interfere with anything. But now, attaching it in the middle of our cycle, well, it just can't be done. Because just at the time they want us to attach the label, we've got to be reaching for the next piece to pre-position it at the head of the machine, ready for processing. Now I ask you. How many

eyes do they think we have? How many things do they expect us to
attend to at the same time? I'd like to see one of them handle the label-
ing of the first piece and the positioning of the second piece at the
same time. It just can't be done. Not when you have to look at both
these things at the same time. Not to mention getting one hand in the
way of the other. I'd like to see them do it. I've been trying it as hard
as I could for a week, and I can't do it.

Case 9 (for role-playing)

Supervisor (John Jones)

One of my best and most experienced operators, Henry Smith, is
having troubles. Maybe he's just getting old and slowing down. Whatever it is, for two straight weeks his production was way below par,
and I know from direct observation that he's been neglecting the
cleaning tasks on his machine. So I placed an instructor with him this
week to help him out. For his own good, as I tried to explain to him at
the time. But he didn't take kindly to the training, I can tell you. He
just about ran the instructor off. Now, what do you do if a fellow rejects the help you provide for him?

Employee (Henry Smith)

By heavens, after all these years I'm being treated by my boss,
John Jones, like a child who doesn't know enough to get in out of the
rain. I had two bad weeks, and he's saddled me with an instructor.
Me—with an instructor who knows about half as much as I do about
the machines. And, in addition to teaching me how to run the machines I can run twice as good as he can, he's teaching me how to clean
them—an operation any idiot could perform with no training at all.

I don't need training; I told that so-called instructor off. Why the
devil doesn't Jones find out what I really need? Why didn't he find out
how lousy the material has been for the past few weeks? Who could
make time processing that junk? And the repairman on my machines
is having trouble with his wife, and he may as well be on the moon for
all the good he's doing me. He never gets around to fix the machines;
he just gripes and fusses in the latrine all the time.

And about the cleaning. By god, I can clean the equipment with
my eyes shut. I'm not neglecting to do it because I don't know how.
It's just that when things go bad, like the materials and the maintenance, the cleaning is just something you have to let go in order to
make any headway at all on production. It's something that can wait—

not forever, of course, but long enough so that I can keep my head above water until these other things are straightened out.

Case 10 (for role playing)

Supervisor (Cal Jamison)

I wish I knew what to do with older operators. They just tend to slow down. It's one of the laws of nature. And we have a devil of a time meeting our labor-cost standards. They can't make the rate, or at least not consistently.

Ruth Boswick is an example. For years—she's been here 25 years at least—she was one of my best assemblers. But the job requires quick movement from place to place, quick hands, and a quick eye. And now she doesn't seem to have the quickness.

But I thought I could help her. I noticed one of the problems was that she still spends a lot of time inspecting the items after she has assembled them. Like an old mother hen, pitting and patting the things before turning them loose. Now I'm a stickler for quality. But the inspection can be done in less time than she takes. I've timed her on that inspection element and she's way over standard. If she is slowing down on the physical part of the job, here is a way to stay even: cut down on the inspection time.

I tried to tell her. I had her in last week. I told her to cut her inspection time, that this is her only hope of keeping production up. But she didn't pay any attention apparently. Her production is still low. I've got to talk to her again.

Employee (Ruth Boswick)

After 25 years with the company, maybe a little more, including quite a few years on the assembly job, I've had my reward. Cal Jamison, my boss, tells me I can't do the job. I've only been doing it for years, you understand. But I can't do the job because I don't make the piece-rate now and again. I admit I'm having my troubles; for some reason I can't keep up the pace over the whole eight hours like I used to. But guess what he advised me to do? Guess what he told me to do just a week ago? Spend less time on quality. I almost fell over when he told me that. Spend less time inspecting the assemblies after putting them together. Imagine that! For 25 years they've been yelling at us about quality, and all at once this fellow Jamison says to forget it.

No sir, I can't do that. I don't know how to do that, and I don't want to know how.

Case 11 (for role playing)

Supervisor (Joe Hines)

I sympathize with my low-seniority machine operators, but above everything else a supervisor has to consider efficiency of operation. So we re-engineered the operator job and took the lowest skilled task out of it and set it up as a separate job. This was the task of filling the magazines or cartridges at each machine with stock to be processed. The stuff feeds automatically into the machine from the cartridge. There's a trick to filling it, but it's easier than the other operating tasks. So, as I said, we sliced it off.

As a result—this was one of the savings in the move—we were able to assign more machines to each operator and to reduce the number of operators. The beauty of it was that we could then offer the cartridge-filling jobs to the excess operators; these would be the men with the lowest seniority from the operator group.

As I say, I sympathize with these fellows. The cartridge-filling job pays less than the operating job, naturally. But we would keep most of them on the payroll, and when a machine operating job came open they would be promoted back to it in line with seniority.

Another advantage of the move was that we could avoid retraining altogether because all of the operators already knew how to fill the cartridges. They had been doing it all along as one of the old operator duties.

Well, as we stand now, the move was made a week ago and no one likes it. Those who remained as operators feel they've been stretched out. Those demoted to cartridge filling are leaving, or, as in the case of Ronald Jennings, one of our newer men, they're soldiering on the job. They're staying way behind the engineered schedule for getting around to the assigned machines. I've decided to talk with all of them, Jennings first, because he's goofing off the worst of all. Three machines were standing idle yesterday because he didn't get the stock to them. I'll tell you this: He'll either make the effort or get out.

Employee (Ronald Jennings)

A week ago I got demoted. I was a machine operator, had been one for six months or so. But a week ago several of us low-seniority operators got put on the job of filling cartridges with stock at the machines. The stock feeds automatically from the cartridge into the machine.

The cartridge-filling job is a new one. It used to be part of the operator's job, but as my boss, Joe Hines, explained, it is not good engineering practice to combine duties of different skill levels into one job. That's what he told us when the change was made. The cartridge-filling task was the lowest skilled part of the operator's job, so they cut it off and made a new and separate job of it. At lower pay, of course.

With my little bit of seniority I was one of the operators who was stuck with the cartridge-filling job. The high-seniority men stayed on the operator job, and we were put out since there were too many of us for the stretched-out operator assignments.

I don't like it. The cartridge filling is below my level of skill. They've "de-skilled" me as well as the job. It pays less and that's important. And it's awfully monotonous. I didn't mind doing it when I was on the machines because it was only part of the job, maybe not a very skilled part, but I like a job where you control the whole works, where the machines are strictly yours, so to speak.

But most of all, I don't know how to keep up on this cartridge-filling job. There is a trick to it I may not have learned. When I did it as a miscellaneous duty I just took my time and got the cartridge filled one way or other. But now when it's a fulltime job in itself and I've got so many machines to get around to, well, it's more than I know how to do.

But I would do it. Some of the others just walked out. I intend to tell Joe Hines off because this whole move is a dirty trick. But I want to stay. I have to work; I can't afford to lose any time looking for something else. And this is a good company, all in all. But I can't keep up. I'm knocking myself out, but I can't keep up.

Appendix
Using Material in This Book

The particular teaching technique used by the instructor should be pertinent to the purpose of the instruction. We start with our objective and fit the technique to it. The general guidelines are rather clear. We know, for instance, that lectures are useful for transmittal of facts but that the intent of changing attitudes or behavior is better served and motivation better achieved if we involve the learner in action.

But there are gradations and mixtures of objectives which argue for a more precise determination of techniques. A partial framework would look like this:

Purpose	*Technique*
To give factual information.	Lecture or reading assignment or both.
To give factual information and assure retention of it.	Lecture or reading assignment or both (emphasis on repetition); quizzing.
To communicate ideas or concepts (requiring insight and understanding).	Lecture and clarifying discussion (questions and answers).
To teach a procedure (intellectual grasp only).	Lecture and clarifying discussion.
To teach the execution of a procedure not involving interpersonal skills (problem solving not related to employee performance, for example).	Lecture, clarifying discussion, modeling (demonstration), and practice through case discussion.
To teach the execution of a procedure involving interpersonal skills (correct-	Lecture, clarifying discussion, modeling, and practice through role-

ing or disciplining an employee, discussing his
progress with him, hear-
ing his complaint or
grievance, for example).

playing (in the "giving"
role for execution of the
procedure; in the "receiving" role for expansion
of perception), and sum-
mary discussion.

If the intent is to evolve the concept or procedure, a participative technique, primarily case discussion, may be indicated at
the very start.

Sometimes the intent is to teach a skill or subprocedure
which is part of the larger unit of learning being undertaken.
For instance, we commonly need to teach fact-gathering as an
aspect of problem solving. A supplementary technique keyed to
this sub-objective might then usefully be put into play; the instructor might in this instance employ the technique of with-
holding information until it is called for by the class.[1]

In the teaching of a decision-making procedure, we may
wish to emphasize the importance of the acceptability of the decision to those employees affected by it and to explore the
means of securing acceptance. We might then move from case
discussion to a role-playing arrangement in which the problem
is presented to the affected employees to permit them to work
through the process of mutual accommodation.[2]

Our list of techniques is a restricted one, deliberately limited to techniques reasonably within the competence of industrial managers and training men who normally serve as conference leaders. It does not include techniques such as game playing, sensitivity training, and other sophisticated teaching
devices whose use requires special training. In addition to this
strong arguments can be opposed to the specific techniques listed. (Lecturing, for instance, appears to be currently out of favor, although it still has its uses and should not be discarded
because of comparatively weak motivational impact.) Never-

---

[1]For a discussion of the "incident process" which requires class members to collect
facts from the conference leader as a major step, see Paul J. W. Pigors and Faith Pigors,
Case Method in Human Relations: the Incident Process (New York: McGraw-Hill, 1961). A
short statement of the steps in the process is made on pp. 149–158.

[2]A prime example of a role-playing case which focuses on acceptability of change is
given in Norman R. F. Maier, Allen R. Solem, and Ayesha A. Maier, *Supervisory and
Executive Development* (New York: Wiley, 1957), pp. 81–98. This volume is a useful guide
for role playing and especially for the use of the multiple role-playing technique.

theless, the idea behind the list is sound: *Tie technique to intent.* Beyond this, an evaluation of effectiveness will lead to necessary variations in approach.

To carry out the intent of this book, which is to teach supervisors and trainers *to use* approaches to skill training, we can take the following as our guiding principles:

- For priming purposes, lectures and demonstration or illustration are most helpful.
- For application and skill development, we need to involve the class members in discussion and practice.

Our stock-in-trade includes learning principles and teaching techniques which are to be applied and certain procedures involving contacts with employees in which skill of execution is to be developed. While it may be possible to elicit the principles, techniques, and procedures from the class through early open discussion of cases, and although we advocate such efforts to a limited extent on the basis of advantages in understanding and retention, we raise serious doubts about the practicality of this arrangement in handling our subject, among them:

- The time spent in eliciting principles and approaches may be prohibitively long. The necessarily limited class time at our disposal is more fruitfully used in a rather direct communication of principles and approaches—without significant sacrifice of understanding, we believe— and a concentration on applications.
- The class instructor must be extremely skillful if he is to move effectively through an open discussion to the development of principles and procedures. In our case, the principles and procedures are known by the instructor; they have evolved through years of experience and research. To permit early participation is to invite the expectation on the part of the class member that his perhaps uninformed opinions are as valid as the instructor's or worth serious consideration by the instructor (else, why should he ask?). And to shape the variety of opinions, good and bad, into a valid and useful principle, technique, or procedure is to run the risk of distorting the class' responses and, in an obvious way, maneuvering the class into a position it really is not headed for.

For the Purpose at Hand

In preparing supervisors and trainers to give effective training to employees, the instructor has the following jobs to perform: (1) to teach the principles of learning and the related training techniques and procedures; (2) to teach the applications of learning principles and related training approaches to the learning problems encountered by employees. The recommended instructional techniques are:

- Explanation of learning principles and explanation, with illustration, of the training approaches which utilize the principles. In certain instances, time allowing, it may be useful to lead the class to the discovery of principles through a discussion of a learning problem.

- Discussion of realistic learning problems presented in the text in the form of opinions or points of view, episodes, or detailed cases. The discussion should be diagnostic in nature, aimed at identifying the relevant principle of learning and the training technique or procedure by which the principle will be used so that learning may proceed efficiently.

- Role playing when the solution to the training problem requires interpersonal skills, as in the discussion of progress with the trainee.

Since discussion and role playing are major vehicles for carrying the training forward, we will examine each in a little greater detail.

Class Discussion

It is obvious by now that we are recommending guided discussion rather than free or unstructured discussion for the handling of our material.[3] The discussion leader is concerned with the *means* of solving learning problems—through identification of the relevant learning principles and training techniques—

---

[3]Conference leadership methods are extensively discussed in Norman R. F. Maier, *Problem-Solving Discussions and Conferences: Leadership Methods and Skills* (New York: McGraw-Hill, 1963). A rationale for the case method is given in Irving J. Lee, *Customs and Crises in Communication* (New York: Harper, 1954), pp. 1–42.

rather than with the answers themselves. The answer may be a correct one or an acceptable one; but if it is reached through guesswork, or trial and error, or mere chance, learning does not occur or is minimal. The leader, having explained the principle and technique, presents cases or situational statements to give the class members practice in application—but in discriminatory application. They must be led to recognize the situations in which the particular learning principle is pertinent and the particular training technique useful, as distinct from those situations which are associated with other principles and respond to other training attacks.

People differ in the extent to which they can apply principles; some see the similarities in situations more readily than others. It is useful to sharpen discriminatory skills through practice in the class—through an examination of numerous problem situations—so that the class members are in better position to transfer their learning to the job and make applications to actual job problems. This purpose of transfer to the job cannot be adequately served by discussion of just a few cases; many are required.

Feedback is an essential requirement in the discussion session if learning is to occur. The instructor should help the class to sort out what will work from what will not work as the class approaches the solution to each problem and should make a summary statement to strengthen the connection between solution and situation.

The precise arrangement for the discussion will depend upon the size of the class and the complexity of the problem addressed. A large class will normally benefit from division into small groups of three to five members unless the problem is so simple as to serve primarily as a teaser. The small-group arrangement permits greater individual participation, which is likely to have a favorable influence on both motivation and development of insight. The problem (situation with questions) is presented to the full group; the group is divided into subgroups; the subgroups tackle the problem; and through a spokesman each subgroup reports to the full group its solution and—this is most important—the basis for it and the means employed to reach it. It is advisable to rotate the role of spokesman and to change the composition of the subgroups. The sub-groups may address themselves to the same questions or, as a variation, may be assigned different questions bearing on the problem. After the reports have been made by the subgroup spokesmen to the reassembled full group, the conference leader may open the discussion to the full group as he moves toward his summarizing statement.

In regard to the subject of discussion, it is a waste of time and a misuse of techniques to crank up a class for a full-blown discussion of trivial or obvious matters. A reasonable rule of thumb is to discuss only those cases which can profitably occupy the class for a minimum of 15 or 20 minutes. Otherwise, a short session of questions and answers will suffice.

Finally, it should be pointed out that transfer of training depends not only on the number of cases presented, as previously mentioned, but also on the nature of the cases. They must realistically represent job-training problems—must be, in a genuine sense, a rich concentration of job experience.

Role Playing

While discussion is largely an intellectual exercise, role playing is a broader experience in the sense of having both intellectual and emotional aspects. Since it involves the carrying-out of procedures or solutions by affected people in direct contact with one another, feelings will inevitably be expressed and responded to.

Role playing is an effective means of teaching the procedures and skills related to interpersonal matters, including the handling of emotional reactions, but only if the class members understand what is expected of them when they take on a role. They frequently misunderstand. The major misconception by the class member is that he is to "be" someone else, that he is to assume a new identity by absorbing a wide range of new characteristics—perceptions, attitudes, values, motivations, temperament traits, and whatever; that if all of these new characteristics are not written in the script he is to invent them; that he is truly expected to play-act.

The resulting role-playing performance is likely to be

strictly a dramatic effort, relying largely on improvisations and well removed from reality. The role becomes an imaginery contrivance which the class member could not possibly sustain in "real life" since it does not represent the expression of characteristics which are validly his.

When a class member is assigned to play a role rather than to deal simply as himself with someone else playing a role, the intent is not to change him but to change the way he acts *by providing him with perceptions of the situation different from his own.* The role, as written, will specify the perceptions and related points of view and, to some extent, the attitudes and background from which the perceptions arise. Within this framework—looking at a situation through the eyes of someone else—he should be and act himself.

Of course, if he takes the role of a supervisor in class and is indeed a supervisor, the transformation presents no great difficulty. He tends to assimilate the designated perceptions rather easily, since they are likely to coincide appreciably with his own in such a situation, and to act himself. But when we ask him to take the role of an employee he supervises (or a role remote from his actual position), he tends to act in a way unnatural to him—as if it were expected. The consequence is that he loses track of the assigned perceptions as they become encrusted with his inventions or he fluctuates erratically between himself and the imagined other fellow, not knowing exactly whom he is supposed to be. If he gains skill in anything, it's in this kind of role playing itself. He may become a good actor, but he does not in such case enlarge his own perceptions and become increasingly sensitive to the views and feelings of employees, which is the benefit he should derive from playing the role of the employee. Nor does he assist the class member taking the supervisory role to develop skill in addressing the assigned type of problem; indeed, he may make the supervisor's task impossible by engaging in foolish and inconsistent behavior which defies orderly or reasoned attack.

In addition to clarifying what he expects of the role player—to take a set of perceptions and certain points of view and act in a natural way on the basis of them—the conference leader should ensure that the role-playing case provides a learning opportunity for all members of the class. That is, he should make efficient use of the technique. This objective is not achieved by having two members perform at the front of the class, supposedly for the enlightenment but usually for the amusement of the rest of the class. To maximize the activity and with it the learning of each individual, for each role-playing case which involves a supervisor and an employee it is helpful to institute a multiple role-playing arrangement using "triads." Under this arrangement, the class is divided into sets of three members each; within each triad, one member is assigned the role of supervisor, one of employee, and the third of observer. By such means, one member is given opportunity to develop supervisory skill in handling problems, another to enlarge his perceptions, and the third to gain insight into the aspects of the interview process which were effective and ineffective. By rotation of the roles, each class member derives all of these benefits.

The major intent of role playing in a supervisory class, of course, is to develop interpersonal skill in solving realistic problems (in our case, learning problems). Individual foremen will need to play the supervisory role many times in order for skill to develop or appreciably improve; numerous role-playing cases should be used. The benefits gained from the other roles should contribute to improvement in the performance of the supervisory role. As the supervisor's perceptions widen and new insights emerge, his interviewing skills should improve.

In addition, the feedback available in the discussion following each role-playing "playout" is important as a means of sharpening skill. In such discussion, a recommended procedure is to call on the observer in each triad to report on how things went—and why—in the interview he observed. Then the leader should open up the discussion to the role players and finally relate the outcomes to the procedures being taught.

In introducing the case, the leader should:

- Explain the recommended procedures which the "foreman" should follow in conducting the interview, procedures which have been proved effective and are to be mastered through role playing.

- Divide the class into triads and distribute the printed role statements: the supervisor's role to one class member, the employee's role to the second, and both roles to the observer.

He should allow each triad enough time to study the material thoroughly and direct the members to start the interview when ready. He should also indicate that the supervisor and employee should never consult each other's role; indeed, should not refer to their own printed roles once the playing has started. He should instruct the observer not to intrude in the interview but simply to observe. It is helpful to provide the observer with a copy of the recommended interview procedure or with a set of related questions which will focus his observations on the crucial aspects of the interview process.

The players should be made to understand that if in the course of the interview they must go beyond the information printed in the role statement, the added information should be consistent with the role rather than contradictory or unrelated. Further, the improvised material should not lead into an unintended problem area.

Of course, a preliminary statement concerning the role-playing technique itself needs to be made by the leader prior to the handling of the first case. He should emphasize what is expected of a class member when he assumes a role so that misunderstanding and resultant misplaying will not occur. It is sometimes useful, as an ice-breaker, to play out the first case by having one member play the role of employee—a role which does not put him "on the spot"—and the rest of the class members serve jointly as the supervisor. With this unthreatening initiation, the class tends to respond freely and to get into the spirit of role playing. The subsequent cases can then be handled by multiple role playing, as suggested.

As with discussions, the role-playing problem must be significant enough to justify the effort. And, of compelling importance, the cases must be realistic enough to assure that the skills developed in role-playing will transfer to the job itself. The role-playing cases in this book are based on experience with the concerns that production foremen express and the problems they are faced with as they attempt to develop competence in their workforce.

Bibliography

Bass, Bernard M., and Vaughan, James A. *Training in Industry, the Management of Learning*. Belmont, California: Brooks/Cole Publishing Company, 1966.

Berelson, Bernard, and Steiner, Gary A. *Human Behavior, an Inventory of Scientific Findings*. New York: Harcourt, Brace and World, 1964.

Bialek, Hilton M.; Taylor, John E.; and Hauke, Robert N. *Instructional Strategies for Training Men of High and Low Aptitude*. Washington: Human Resources Research Organization, 1973.

Bienvenu, Bernard J. *New Priorities in Training*. New York: American Management Association, Inc., 1969.

Bilodeau, Edward A., ed. *Acquisition of Skill*. New York: Academic Press, 1966.

Broadwell, Martin M. *The Supervisor and On-The-Job Training*. Reading, Mass.: Addison-Wesley Publishing Company, Inc., 1969.

Campbell, John P.; Dunnette, Marvin D.; Lawler, Edward E., III; and Weick, Karl E., Jr. *Managerial Behavior, Performance, and Effectiveness*. New York: McGraw-Hill Book Company, 1970.

Craig, Robert L., and Bittel, Lester R., eds. *Training and Development Handbook*. New York: McGraw-Hill Book Company, 1967.

Elliott, Ralph D. "Teaching and Training with PSI." *The Clemson University Review of Industrial Management and Textile Science* 14, No. 2, (1975): 61–67.

Fleishman, Edwin A., ed. *Studies in Personnel and Industrial Psychology*. Rev. ed. Homewood, Ill.: The Dorsey Press, 1967.

Gagne, Robert M. *The Conditions of Learning*. New York: Holt, Rinehart and Winston, 1965.

Gilmer, B. von Haller, ed. *Industrial Psychology*. 2d ed. New York: McGraw-Hill, 1966.

Hamblin, A. C. *Evaluation and Control of Training*. Maidenhead, Berkshire, England: McGraw-Hill Book Company Limited, 1974.

Homme, Lloyd, and Tosti, Donald. *Behavior Technology: Motivation and Contingency Management*. Units One and Two, Three and Four, and Student's Manual. San Rafael, Calif.: Individual Learning Systems, Inc., 1971.

Hughes, J. L. *Programed Instruction for Schools and Industry*. Chicago: Science Research Associates, Inc., Publishers, 1962.

Kirkpatrick, Donald L., ed. *Evaluating Training Programs.* Madison, Wisc.: American Society for Training and Development, 1975.

Lee, Irving J. *Customs and Crises in Communication.* New York: Harper & Brothers, Publishers, 1954.

Lee, Irving J., and Lee, Laura L. *Handling Barriers in Communication.* New York: Harper & Brothers, Publishers, 1957.

Lovin, Bill C., and Casstevens, Emery Reber. *Coaching, Learning, and Action.* New York: American Management Association, Inc., 1971.

Lumsdaine, A. A., and Glaser, Robert, eds. *Teaching Machines and Programmed Learning.* Washington: National Education Association of the United States, 1960.

Luthans, Fred, and Kreitner, Robert. *Organizational Behavior Modification.* Glenview, Ill.: Scott, Foresman and Company, 1975.

McGehee, William, and Thayer, Paul W. *Training in Business and Industry.* New York: John Wiley & Sons, Inc., 1961.

Mager, Robert F. *Preparing Instructional Objectives.* Palo Alto, Calif.: Fearon Publishers, Inc., 1962.

Mager, Robert F., and Pipe, Peter. *Analyzing Performance Problems or 'You Really Oughta Wanna.'* Belmont, Calif.: Fearon Publishers, 1970.

Maier, Norman R. F. *Problem-solving Discussions and Conferences: Leadership Methods and Skills.* New York: McGraw-Hill Book Company, Inc., 1963.

Maier, Norman R. F. *Psychology in Industrial Organizations.* 4th ed. Boston: Houghton Mifflin Co., 1973.

Maier, Norman R. F.; Solem, Allen R.; and Maier, Ayesha A. *Supervisory and Executive Development: a Manual for Role Playing.* New York: John Wiley & Sons, Inc., 1957.

Melton, Arthur W., ed. *Categories of Human Learning.* New York: Academic Press, 1964.

Mikulas, William L. *Behavior Modification: An Overview.* New York: Harper & Row, Publishers, 1972.

Newcomb, Theodore M.; Turner, Ralph H.; and Converse, Philip E. *Social Psychology.* New York: Holt, Rinehart and Winston, 1965.

Odiorne, George S. *Training by Objectives.* New York: The Macmillan Company, 1970.

On-the-Job Training. Prime VIII. New York: American Management Association, Inc., 1965.

Pigors, Paul J. W., and Pigors, Faith. *Case Method in Human Relations: the Incident Process.* New York: McGraw-Hill Book Company, Inc., 1961.

Porter, Lyman W., and Steers, Richard M. "Organizational, Work, and Personal Factors in Employee Turnover and Absenteeism." *Psychological Bulletin* 80, No. 2, (1973): 151–176.

Seymour, W. Douglas. *Industrial Skills.* London: Pitman, 1966.

Skinner, B. F. *The Technology of Teaching.* New York: Appleton-Century-Crofts, 1968.

Stokes, Paul M. *Total Job Training.* New York: American Management Association, Inc., 1966.

Tiffin, Joseph, and McCormick, Ernest J. *Industrial Psychology.* 5th ed. Englewood Cliffs, N.J.: Prentice-Hall, Inc., 1965.

Index

179